Driven Obsession© 2018 by Gerald Johnson Jr. All rights reserved.
Published by Vantage Point Publishing
Indianapolis, IN 46205

No part of this publication may be reproduced or transmitted in any form or by any means, electronic or mechanical, including photocopy, or any information storage and retrieval system, without permission from the publisher. The only exception is a brief quotation in printed reviews.

Limit of Liability/Disclaimer of Warranty: While the publisher and author have used their best efforts in preparing this book, they make no representations or warranties with respect to the accuracy or completeness of the contents of this book and specifically disclaim any implied warranties of merchantability or facilities for a particular purpose. No warranty may be created or extended by any persons. The advice or strategies herein may not be suitable for your situation. You should consult with a professional where appropriate. Neither the publisher nor author should be liable for any loss of profit or any other incidental damages, including but not limited to special, consequential, or other damages.

This is a work of fiction. Names, characters, businesses, places, events and incidents are either the products of the author's imagination or used in a fictitious manner. Any resemblance to actual persons, living or dead, or actual events is purely coincidental.

ISBN 978-1-943159-18-5

LCCN 2018908996

Acknowledgements

I know the general idea behind the way that most acknowledgements are done, but for this book I want to go a different route. I want to start off with thanking those few who did the best 2 things that can be done for a writer and it wasn't hard and it was compromised of two things... Money and time. They all took a little money to purchase my work and they took a little time to read it. I want to Thank you all first. As a writer, I've always shared tidbits of my work here and there to a select few people through the years, and it was always their Words of encouragement that kept me growing as an artist. As a published author, it was a surprise to get the positive response that I did after the release of Tainted 1; granted I didn't get a lot of written feedback in the form of stars and reviews, but my inbox has been struck on several occasions with rewarded glee. Thank you all... not only for the money spent and the time used but more so for your honesty because that goes even further for a writer. I've continued to grow and learn in the hopes that each time someone picks up one of my pieces of work they are Entertained. I want to feel that with each piece I leave them wanting more of me... more of what I have to offer... more of what and who I am. Thank you all... Thank you for allowing me into your lives but thank you more for joining me in my worlds because without you all, truthfully, I may as well just go back to sporadically sharing things on my Facebook fan pages. You've shown me that I've made the right choice, and that my little call to action rings true:

I am making new Fans one Reader at a time.

As I sit here writing this, I am wearing the "GRJ Customs" t-shirt that my brother made and gave to me on my 45th birthday; most people who know me know I don't celebrate, but I wear this shirt with pride. For me it serves as a reminder that my family means the world to and that no matter what I will always be there for them. It means that for me, my love for them knows No boundaries... No limits. I have spent many nights in the dark crying and hoping that I have kept my promise to my Father to be the best son to my Mother and the best brother to my Sister and Brother... and through the years I've questioned and doubted but they've remained at my side and I'll never leave theirs. We are bound together for life, and I continue to hope that the love and support from them I've always returned. The one thing that I know above and beyond all else is this: Kia Johnson will always be my little sister, Antavio Johnson will always be my baby brother, Glenda Johnson will always be our mothering unit and without the three of them I wouldn't be the Gerald Robert Johnson, Jr. that I am. Thank you's all around to my family, Mi Familia... I love you all from the bottom of my heart.

They say that a man without children has no one to pass his life's knowledge on to, and I've been blessed with a few. Some are dipped in my blood and others are just guilty by association, but I love them all. The one thing that I'd want them to know and carry away from me is that life is what you make of it... the good, the bad and the ugly all have a place in their lives and the lessons that they take away from each moment is how they will grow as a person. I want them to know that it is never too late to learn something new or to try something new as long as it leads them off into a positive direction. I want them to know that the world owes them Nothing, but it offers them Everything so live life to the fullest. My kids mean the world to me and even though me may be separated by time and space I am always but a heartbeat away. To those who have my heart and soul, all of the children who are a part of my life: Aleya (my cook competition), Nichelle (my oldest), Brianna (my favorite soldier), Le'Keva (my drama queen), Tyrell (my artist), Terrin (my movie aficionado), Gerald III (my awesome gamer), Tra'Von (my mini me), and Tirrek (my little Texan)... I have to add in my grandchildren to this mix of kiddos, so, we start with my two oldest, Isaiah and Emma, and then we add in my lil bear, Nichari. My nieces Tranique, Taleaha, Phoenix, and the lil bug Trinity, and my nephews Javion and Elite... All of you have me in your corners for life and I love you all.

There's been these two ladies helping to keep my pathway clear especially these last couple of years and I want to take a moment to thank them both. Believe it or not, I met Anita almost 20 years ago thanks to the internet and a chat server called Mirc, now for a lot of us this was just after AOhell went to crap and the internet was still pretty much dialup (aka: slow as hell). Late nights after work on a desktop that seemed fresh out of the stone ages I'd login and sit around downloading music and movies and talking to people ALL over the world, and she happened to be one. For the longest time people would get to know you by aliases and nicknames and back then mine was either Mr.De^Vil (who a lot of people confused with Mr. de Mil) or Mr. DeVille (who actually has his own story). Ours is a crazy history that has somehow managed to survive year after year. She is one of my bestest of best friends putting up with some of my more trying times and helping me walk away with most of my skin and little of my insanity intact. Thank you for showing me that even a guy like me has a little good inside. Thank you for showing me that I am worthy and that I'm not always the bad guy. I love you to death. Thank you... Thank you... THANK YOU! And then there's Ms. Dawn Rivers, she saved my literary Life and all she did was approach me with a question that changed my way of thinking where my writing was concerned.

"So, what are you going to do with all of your writing?" and this was within two minutes of introducing herself to me. Dawn put the bug of wanting to elevate my writing, to make it more than what it was... to push it beyond being a messy first draft and create a piece of work that demanded to be published and read by the masses. She helped to that next rung in the ladder of being a writer; that's being a published author, but she told me to NEVER stop being a writer... Never lose my love for the words. She is my literary Jiminy Cricket, and she's become another of my bestest of best friends. She's one that I can talk to about anything and a member of my family. I love you to death too and Thank You for everything that you've added to my life.

    There's one more group of people who I'd like to stop a moment and thank. Some I've known for a lifetime and some have been recently added into this small circle of people I call my Friends. These are those people I could be dead, blind and mute and still pick them out of a crowd. These are people who I know got my back and they know I'm right there for them no matter what. These are those select few who have given me support and guidance over the course of time, and for that I am greatly appreciative. I want to start with Cori Lynne and Karra Lyn, I don't know who bought the first and who bought the second books of Tainted 1 but they both didn't hesitate the moment it became available. Within hours after purchase they were both calling and demanding answers to questions and wanting to know when book 2 would be out. I got cussed at a lot, but it was great because they let me know that Tainted needed a second book. Thank you ladies for always being there you have my love and respect forever, and I believe that you are my greatest fans. To Joe Judge and Oliver Bostic, my two big brothers, and the two men that I've known and loved as my brothers for the better part of 40+ years... Two men who probably got enough on me to write their own books. The years have been crazy but no matter what you two have me in your corners no matter what. To Ms. Melinda Sue (yes, I know it's really Ann) we've come a long way, but you know that you mean the world to me. You've helped me in ways with your thoughts and our political arguments that keeps me sane at times. You are my needed conversation and we have a way of talking about everything under the sun that always amazes me. Thank you for being that one who constantly asks me about my crazy life and all of the people in it. You have managed to be a light when I was very sufficed with my darkness. There are a few more that I want to give out honorary shout outs to... Elaine "North Florida" Wood, in a short time I've come to know another writer who shares my passion for writing... I want to wish the best with all of your writings and know that my door is always open for our literary sparring. I'll see you at the top of the charts... just don't forget about me when you get there. To Tima Boyd, she's been a sounding board for me for many, many years and always one of the first people to tell me that I need to stop hiding the talent that I have and show it to the world. Well, Tima, I'm showing it to the world and I'm hoping that they will see in me what you've always said you see in me. Thank you so very much for always being there. And to Ms. Jennifer Love, she has become one of those fans that's always hungry for more. She's my kind of fan because not only does she look forward to my new works, but she shares them with her mom... The two for one deal yaaaaa! Thank you very, very much for being their asking, requesting, and at times demanding new things to read. Like I said, my kind of fan!

    Thank you all for being there for me. My journey is just at its meager beginnings with so much more on the horizon. The dream is to one day be on the New York Times best sellers list, and with the support I've been getting... that's no longer just a dream it is Inevitable. Thank you again and always. There are so many more and I hope that I continue to entertain you all.

YOU ALL HAVE MY LOVE AND RESPECT!

As always, I want to dedicate this book to my Dad, Gerald R Johnson, Sr... I think if you were here you would understand and applaud me for these two books. I love you
Semper Fi!!!

And to my mom, aka Ma... aka the Mothering Unit... aka the best person I know and even though she's not allowed to read my books, her eyes are too young for this stuff, she is and has always been My BIGGEST Fan. I love you, Glenda J.

Driven Obsession

Table of Contents

Table of Contents..
Chapter 1: The Accusation...
Chapter 2: That First Encounter...
Chapter 3: A Fantasy Realized..
Chapter 4: The Hot Seat..
Chapter 5: Meeting Again..
Chapter 6: Frail Memories...
Chapter 7: A Broken Smile..
Chapter 8: Time With His Princess..
Chapter 9: Another Lesson to Teach.......................................
Chapter 10: Do You Know your Wife.....................................
Chapter 11: The Book Tour..
Chapter 12: "He Should Have Told Me."................................
Chapter 13: The Pawns are in Place......................................
Chapter 14: Mommy's Asleep, Kennadey...............................
Chapter 15: One More to Go..
Chapter 16: "Everything We Thought is Wrong.".....................
Chapter 17: Unwinding the Mystery......................................
Chapter 18: Filling in the Missing Pieces................................
Chapter 19: The Reunion...
Chapter 20: Full Circle and a New Story to Come....................
About the Author..

Chapter 1: The Accusation

He'd been sitting for the last hour or so with his head down into the palms of his hands thinking. Everything was nothing more than a blur of images that continued to flash through his brain and before his closed eyes that ran on a continuous loop that was giving him the worst headache.

"Can somebody please tell me what the hell is going on?" he sighed deeply before slamming the palms of his hands down upon the table.

Graylin Cross was tired of sitting in this uncomfortably wooden chair at this small metal table inside this small room for however long he'd been sitting. All he could think of was the fact that he'd been dragged from his home in the middle of the night with some tough acting cop pulling at his arm, forcing him into the backseat of his patrol car, and no one said a word to him of why. He could hear the one cop's partner telling him to shut the fuck up as they drove off with the entire neighborhood watching the spectacle.

"I'm getting tired of sitting here staring at myself in this goddamn mirror," he stood walking towards the large one-way glass pressing his face against attempting to look through. "Either tell me what's going on... or let me go. I'm giving you five minutes and then I'm demanding my lawyer."

The door's hinges screeched as the it was pushed inward, and Graylin remained at the mirrored window turning to watch the two plainly dressed people walk in. The man was a bit heavy set with a gray suit on that seemed to squeeze uncomfortably at his pudgy body. The graying hair, what little of it there was, was combed over the top of his head to somewhat cover the balding crown and hung in wisps along the sides. The man's bushy eyebrows were almost all white hanging over blue eyes that still held a sparkle of life. Wrinkles decorated his aged and over tanned face with crow's feet deeply pressed against the edges of his eyes as well as at his lips as well the furrows on his forehead.

The woman following him in was drastically younger; so much so that he wondered if she was fresh from cadet school and tossed in with this aging dinosaur to one day take his place. Her eyes were sharp, brown and dissecting him at a rate that he felt violated. Her suit was tight as well, but in a more pleasing manner that he had to force his eyes from staring as she walked towards him. Her long dark hair was pulled up and tied off in a ponytail that bounced with each step, and her face; as pretty as it was, was only lightly made up giving her an almost paled demeanor.

Graylin stepped away from the window as she stepped up towards him. She didn't scare him, which he was sure was the point of her walking up on him, but he definitely didn't like her being so close. Walking around the table he dropped his head and shook it as the man pulled out a chair and made himself comfortable.

"Have a seat, Mr. Cross," he waved at the chair across from him, "please."

"Can you tell me what the hell is going on?" Graylin grabbed the chair pulling it back before dropping down into it. "I'm sick of sitting here and…"

"Mr. Cross," the officer interrupted, "my name is Detective Erick Marcum and my partner is Detective Ilissa Abraham. If I can get you to calm down a bit I'm sure we can figure out what's going on so that we can get you out here as soon as possible."

"Get me out of here," Graylin repeated. "Look, not trying to be disrespectful, but I've already said that you people have five minutes to either let me in on this big secret as to why I'm here or get me my goddamn lawyer because I'm tired of waiting."

Marcum sat staring at him with an unnerving smile that reaffirmed that he was unconcerned with any threats that Graylin wanted to spout. He ran his fingers through his thinned-out hair waiting for the other man to finally calm himself enough so that they could begin this process. Glancing over his shoulder he nodded to his partner who had posted her back to the mirror and watching the little melodrama with very little interest.

Marcum thumbed the edge of the folder he'd dropped on the table as he waited. This was the part of the job that he enjoyed because it would let him know the personality of the "accused" sitting across from him. Silently he did a quick assessment of Graylin Cross while letting him stew a bit longer. The younger man was a good-looking kid, not necessarily a model type, but definitely a kid in his near sixty-year-old eyes. He was in his early to mid-thirties, and from his clothing he was a man not hurting for money, but still moderately dressed. In his notes prior to stepping into the interrogation room he'd written down a few descriptive notes of the man being a black male with brown eyes, a little over six feet tall and he'd guessed his weight to be about the mid-200's. As a bit of a side note, Marcum had written down that Cross was a bit of a nondescript fellow; someone who could easily fit into or even disappear into a crowd.

The younger man was eyeballing him his brow furrowed and undoubtedly unappreciative of his current situation; which Marcum knew from experience, was about to worsen. He was in decent shape based on the form fitting shirt stretched across his chest and around his arms, and he was not a bad looking man thanks to how his partner was openly appraising him.

Marcum smiled as he flipped the folder open as he prepared for the next part of the sparring match. "Are you quite done, Mr. Cross?" he asked without the least bit of concern for the man across the table.

Graylin stares bounced between the sitting man and the standing woman who had been sent into this small room to intimidate him. Taking a deep breath and popping his knuckles he decided that it was time to just play this little game out to see exactly where this bullshit was leading. He hadn't done shit wrong and he could tell that his threat to call in a lawyer didn't faze anyone in the room, but little did they know he was prepared to call his lawyer to come get him up out here.

"Can we get this shit over with?" he remained defiant. "I want to go home."

"Do you know Elise Mannsen, Mr. Cross?" Marcum asked dryly.

"Yea, I know her," Graylin leaned forward over the table. "Why? Is she alright? Has something happened to her?"

His concern for the woman was not what Marcum was expecting. As he looked into the man's eyes, he could see that the concern was genuine. Wiping his lips with his hand he sat for a moment to reconsider his approach.

"That's exactly what we're here to determine," Abraham responded folding her arms across her chest.

"Ok..." Graylin sat back away from the table once again going from the man to the woman as they both held on to their stone-faced visage. "What the hell is that supposed to mean?"

"Simply this, Mr. Cross," Marcum began shuffling through the papers and photos in the folder. "How well would you say that you know Ms. Mannsen? Would you say that you're just friends or... are you good friends?"

"What the hell are you getting at?" his voice raised as he glared across the table. "I am so not in the mood for anymore of this bullshit, so either spit it out or I'm walking out. You brought me here without any provocation and I'm done with this."

The first picture slid across the table almost made him vomit. The woman in the pictured was beaten and bruised making her face unrecognizable. Her eyes were black and swollen to the point of being closed, her nose looked broken and cocked off center of her face and it too was bleeding profusely. Her lips had been beaten and looked easily twice their normal size and split leaving the bottom of her face soaked in blood and saliva. The next few pictures that the detective slid over to him showed the woman from different angles but all showing off the gruesome injuries in differing lights. Graylin felt his stomach churning as he shoved the pictures back across the table.

"What the fuck is that?"

"You tell us, Mr. Cross," Abraham interjected as she stepped up to the table. "Look at the pictures… what the hell do you see?"

"Who the fuck is that?" Graylin was nearly hysterical.

"What?" Marcum shoved the first picture back across the table. "Do you recognize her, or maybe this will help."

The next picture choked him up. Elise was looking up at him looking as beautiful as the day he'd first seen her. Long, black hair draped over her shoulder with that one part of her bangs draped over her left eye. Her icy, blue eyes were one of the most alluring features of her gorgeous face they always drew him in hypnotizing him to her every whim. She was the kind of beautiful that he had always referred to as being classic; meaning, she never had to wear any kind of make-up to look stunning. She reminded him of a porcelain doll with her flawless skin, and the arch of her eyebrows and the fullness of her lips excited him beyond words.

"Those pictures are not…" Graylin stuttered. "That's not Elise, is it?"

"You don't recognize her?" Abraham asked. "She doesn't look the same after the workout you put on her, does she?"

"Wait," Graylin jumped up from the table, "you think I did… that? I didn't do that shit… I wouldn't do nothing like that. I wouldn't ever hurt her like that…Even after all of the shit we've been through, I... I still."

"You still what, Mr. Cross?" Abraham was glaring, and the look was obvious.

"The question remains, Mr. Cross," Marcum said staring across the table at the traumatized man trying to ascertain what he was seeing, "how well do you kn--"

"She's my wife," Graylin yelled. "My ex-wife. I would never… fuck."

Graylin dropped back down into the chair but pushed it from the table refusing to allow his eyes to fall on the two pictures. He sat fighting the burning urges of his stomach to empty right there on the room floor by taking deep breaths hoping against hope that the extra oxygen would calm him. His hands were holding on the sides of the chair's seat so hard that his knuckles were turning gray and his fingernails hurt digging into the wood. Tears filled his eyes and he kept shaking his head refusing to believe what he'd seen.

"You're lying," he mumbled. "No, you're lying. That's not her. I just saw her a few days ago and she was perfectly fine. You're lying… why are you fucking lying to me?"

"Wait, did you just say that you spoke with Ms. Mannsen a couple of days ago?" Abraham glanced over at her partner before standing up.

"No, Detective, I saw my ex-wife morning before I left going out of town to an authors' convention in Atlanta," he swallowed hard still trying to calm his stomach.

"What day was that, Mr. Cross?" Marcum looked at the pictures and then across at the hysterical man. He was beginning to wonder if they'd have to call in the emergence response team to keep this man from passing out.

"Shit, that was Tuesday, and I didn't even get back into town until maybe an hour before those to assholes forced me into their car."

"You've been out of town for the last week?" Abraham responded incredulously. "Can you prove that? Do you have a ticket or something to show that you were out of town?"

"Why was this never mentioned?" Marcum glanced up at Abraham as she shrugged her shoulders. "Do you have proof of this trip?"

Reaching into his back pocket Graylin pulled out his wallet and reached into it taking out the return ticket stub he'd stuffed in there for his personal scrapbook. He threw over towards the table. He wiped his eyes and watched as the two cops glared at the ticket stub and then at him. He was shaking as the images of her beaten face kept flashing before his eyes.

"Had you told her that you were headed out of town?" Abraham asked.

"No, I hadn't told her shit about my plans. She wasn't even supposed to be near me," his voice was a mere whisper, "I had a restraining order against her and she wasn't supposed to come within a hundred yards of me. That's why she was there at my house; she wanted to bitch at me about it. You can ask my neighbors, there were quite a few of them who saw us arguing at my front door."

"Dammit," Abraham walked around the table to stand directly in front of him. "Mr. Cross, you filed for a restraining order against Ms. Mannsen?"

"Two months ago," he was trying to look around her at the pictures. "About two months ago after I came home, and she was in my bedroom half naked, talking about she wanted to make things right between us. When I told her that I wanted her to leave she got violent and I had to call you guys. They took pictures of the fucking scratch marks and the black eye she gave me. My publicist was there too, she was downstairs."

"Damn, this changes a lot," Abraham's lip curled up in disgust.

"What the hell is going on here?" Graylin stared from one to the other.

"Please excuse us for a moment, Mr. Cross," Marcum had pushed his seat back from the table, "we need to check on a few things and it appears that we may need to get your… ex-wife… back in here for some further questioning."

"Did she say that I did that to her?" Graylin was standing as the two detectives moved towards the door. "This shit ain't the first time, but that bitch knows I wouldn't hit her. I don't fucking hit women… Period. She fucking knows that because she'd tried to get me to hit her stupid ass a few times when we were together."

"Please calm down, and we'll be right back."

Marcum didn't stop walking out the door and waited as Abraham closed it behind her. He stood in the hall looking around and running his fingers through his thinning hair. The information from the aggravated man in the interrogation room was completely unsettling leaving him with more questions than he currently had answers for.

"This is some bullshit we've stepped into," he said more to himself than his female partner. "I hate domestic shit."

"Looks like we've been lied to, Partner," Abraham stated the obvious.

"Yea," Marcum shook his head, "no doubts about that, but there's still something all fucked up here. I think we need to keep pushing this one but send a car out to pick her ass up. And, have someone pull up that goddamn restraining order... I can't believe the shit that's being missed on this."

"Gotcha," Abraham walked leaving Marcum standing there watching Cross pace the floor in the interrogation room.

Chapter 2: That First Encounter

"Mr. Cross, Mr. Cross," he'd come to love hearing his name screamed out over a crowd. "Will you be writing anymore books to add to this current series?"

"That's a damn good question," he smiled looking out over the throng of people crowded around the small wooden table covered with his most current book. "My publisher and I were discussing that very thing just a few days ago, but I'm still unsure which direction I'll be going. I am currently working on a couple of new projects, but nothing's jumped out as my next to-be-competed project."

"Do you plan to continue writing about serial killers, or have you decided to jump off into a totally different genre all together?"

"Well," Graylin smiled as everyone seemed to be hanging on his every word, "as I've said, I am working on a few new things, there are a couple of new psychological thrillers in the bunch, but I have been dabbling with a couple of science fiction stories which is something I haven't done in years."

The questions kept coming and he continued answering; over the course of the last couple of years he'd become quite comfortable talking to the press. He loved the questions especially those he'd get from the actual readers because they always gave him new material for anything he'd be working on. The atmosphere in the small book store was pleasant and the owners were extremely delighted with the turn out and the number of new purchases of the Cross soon to be best seller. His publicist had set up this book signing because he'd frequented the store often, and he'd have to remember to thank her for stepping up.

Slowly the hubbub died down to a gentle roar of the book readers holding conversations amongst themselves. Graylin was a little thankful as he finally had to opportunity to sit down to begin this long day of signing books and keeping up a smile that was locked upon his lips and stretching his face. He looked back at the young lady standing off to the side of him and nodded his head as a gesture of beginning the second part of this show and she stepped forward as he sat and pulled himself up to the table.

"Ok, ok everyone," she was waving her hand to get everyone's attention. "May I have your attention please? Mr. Cross is ready to begin the signing so if you would… please form a single line to the left of the table. We do ask that your requests be short because as you can see Mr.

Cross will be at this for a while."

Graylin and everyone chuckled as Aura Daniels continued to go through the pre-requisites of the signing. He had a bad habit of staring at the younger woman whenever she wasn't looking; she was quite a beautiful woman that he'd often wondered if his publisher was up to no good where the publicist was concerned. She was rather short but the heels she always wore gave her the height she commanded, her complexion was like opening a Werther's Original and seeing that creamy caramel up close and personal with dark brown eyes that could stop any man mid-sentence. It was times like these he loved the most because she was standing with her back to him giving him the perfect angle to move his eyes up her slender legs that disappeared beneath to the too short skirt but leading him right to her ass he'd had dreams of touching in more ways than one.

We're going to have a long talk about this one, Mishelle, he mumbled as the girl turned and smiled.

"They're ready for you, Mr. Cross."

"Thank you, Aura," he said picking up the first of the five pens laid out for him to use.

Popping his fingers and looking down the line of people Graylin smiled. Today was a great showing of people here to see him and get his new book, and that was always thrilling. He glanced down at the table was stacked with copies and he knew that it was going to be a long day as he waved his first fan up and accepted the receipt for the book purchase.

"I've been a fan since your very first book, Mr. Cross," the man looked like he should be home playing dungeons and dragons or Magic: The Gathering, and this made Graylin smile.

"Oh yea?" he said opening the book to where he'd sign. "What was your favorite part?"

"I loved the fight scene between Diana and Captain Morgano," the man quickly answered. "It was like being right there as she weaved herself around a much larger man until she was able to get through his guard. The way that you described the blade slipping through his flesh and piercing his spine... wow."

A real fan of his writing. Graylin was completely beside himself. It had been a long time since anyone had brought up any of his work prior to him being signed to a major label, and for it to be about his lady pirate Diana Linde only solidified that he was always meant to be a writer. He could sit here and talk to this one man all day, but he got the man's name and wrote him something special to thank him for making the start of his day extremely special.

The line moved slow but talking to the people only seemed to get better. Each one reminded him of something from his past books. He wasn't one of those writers who would go and put out ten to twelve books within a year, but little did most people know that he had enough books in his coffers busy throughout the year. He did like for his people, his fans, to be itching and begging for something new and thus he'd put out two books per year.

Aura was doing her job going from fan to fan asking them for their opinions about the new book's cover and for new story ideas. She was definitely good with people and she kept a group of them involved as the line continued to crawl forward; he'd have to talk to Mishelle about getting the young lady some kind of incentive raise to keep her motivated. What pleased him most about her was that she was always looking out for new venues for him to do his book signings, and she was getting rather creative.

"Excuse me, Mr. Cross," Mrs. Beasley, one of the owners was at his side.

"Yes, Ma'am?"

"I'd like for you to meet someone, Sir," she smiled pressing her hand in the back of the young lady at her side trying to push her forward. "I know that you're in the middle of signing, but this is Elise, she's been a big supporter of our little shop, and she was one of the first to purchase your very first book that we carried. She's been a huge fan ever since and pretty much begged me to introduce her to you."

Graylin apologized to the next person in line asking for just a moment and then he turned. His eyes felt as if they were about to pop from their sockets as he stared up at the young lady standing beside the elderly woman smiling down at him; he stood almost turning over the table of books and extended his hand.

"Hi," he responded trying to catch his breathing. "Graylin Cross."

"Yes, you are," she almost shrieked as she reached out taking his hand and shaking it frantically. "I'm... I'm Elise, Elise Mannsen, and I cannot believe that I'm finally meeting you. Mr. Cross, I am your biggest fan... I know that you hear that a lot, but I am being so for real right now."

The heels she wore made her look as tall as he and they were staring into one another's eyes. Smoldering coals of liquid ice burned into his skull as he tried to find his footing before tripping and falling all over the woman. She was more than beautiful and the more he looked at her the more he found he couldn't take his eyes off of her. Her long dark hair hung loose down to the middle of her back. Her lips weren't full but spread into a full smile had him smitten.

"I'm so glad that you're here," he choked out before stepping back to pull a chair over to his table. "Please, sit and we can get to know each other while I sign some more books."

Graylin couldn't help but to drop his eyes and watch as her breasts bounced up and down as she squealed and hopped around like a cheerleader clapping her hands. Her excitement was his excitement as he wished he could excuse himself from the room and run off to make a couple of adjustments, but he held the back of the chair waiting for her to sit down. He watched as the hem of the skirt she was wearing rode up her legs as she eased into the seat, and he had a bird's eye view down the front of her top and he smiled at his fortunes.

As he took his seat and turned back towards the crowd, he caught the sideways glance of Aura at his guest. The beautiful redhead had no cares of showing that she did not care for the other woman sitting next to him, and he grinned. Picking up his pen he waved for his next fan to step forward. The woman was a little older, but she still looked nice and she tried to plaster an amicable smile on her face as she slid her book across the table.

"What got you into writing about psychos and killers?" Elise asked as she smiled at the woman now openly glaring at her.

"I don't really know how to answer that one," Graylin smiled as he scribbled the woman's name and a small message to her before scratching his name boldly across the page. "I guess you can say that I have a slight love for the macabre. I was a kid who grew up on old fashion slasher movies and a man who loves crime dramas… so at some point I decided to bring them together. I studied serial killers and even did a little studying into split personalities and manic psychosis.

"It was fun."

"Now why do I not find that too hard to believe about you?" Elise responded.

They laughed and continued talking as the next fan walked up and begged him for a hug and a kiss. Graylin stood and leaned over the table to give the woman a big hug before pressing his lips to her cheek. He was quickly caught up in the whirlwind of her excitement as she hung on to his neck and pulling his face down towards her exposed cleavage.

Turning his head, he could see Aura shaking hers as she stood off some ways from the floor show with her arms folded across her chest. He shrugged his shoulders as if to let her know that he had no control over his fans, but the smile on his face told that he loved the attention. Elise was sitting there laughing with the over excited woman as she held her captive into her chest swinging back and forth keeping him smothered in her very abundant breasts.

"Ma'am?" Aura finally stepped forward and placed a hand on the woman's arm. "Could you please release Mr. Cross so that we can continue with the rest of the book signing?"

"I love this man," the woman squealed as she squeezed his head into her breasts once more. "I have wanted to meet you for the longest."

"What's your name?" Graylin mumbled from her cleavage.

"Monique," she was kissing the top of his head. "Monique Taylor, and I am one of your biggest fans. I even have a fanpage set up in your honor on Facebook."

"I'll have to find it and check it out," Graylin was laughing as he felt Aura pulling at the woman's arms to release him. "You'll have to release my head and write it down for me."

The woman finally released his head and attempted to kiss him once more, but he dropped down into his seat just out of her reach. Her book was sitting on the table and he snatched it up signing it as Aura leaned over asking if he was alright. He passed the woman her book and a business card for her to write down the Facebook page as he let his publicist know that he was fine. He grinned looking over at Elise who was still laughing almost uncontrollably.

"Why do you continue to make things so difficult for me?" Aura huffed and stomped back off to where she'd been standing. "Ms. Rivers don't pay me enough to keep babysitting you."

"I'd be worried if I knew you didn't love me," Graylin blew her a kiss before resuming the book signing once more.

Elise was a tornado of questions and as he wrote he kept up. It was so refreshing to just sit and talk to someone who seemed to really know him beyond just his books. From his birthday to where he'd been born right down to the little tidbit of trivia he'd give about his being born the day man landed on the moon. She didn't shy away from any of his questions about where she'd been born, and she was quick about telling him all about her dysfunctional family.

They fed off of one another and their stories just filled the book store even as the fans brought their own stories to the mix. Graylin had never had a book signing as exciting as this one and he was working out a way to thank Elise for bringing more to his day. One more look at Aura and he knew he'd have to sit her down soon and talk about this new attitude she was showcasing in front of his fans.

The final fan in the line was walking away extremely happy, and before he could turn to address the woman sitting beside him, she was sliding over her book. Her smile was intoxicating, and her eyes were hypnotic as he opened the book to his signature page.

"So," he licked his lips, "who would you like for me to make this out to?"

"I'm going to boldly step out on a limb and say... *to my future wife, Elise, I look forward to seeing what tomorrow holds for us.*"

And that is exactly what he wrote.

Chapter 3: A Fantasy Realized

"So," he was smiling ear to ear just hearing her voice on the phone, "when are you coming to see me?"

Graylin was stretched out on the hotel bed in nothing but a tank top t-shirt and his boxer briefs. He was puffing on a cigar with a glass of brandy in his free hand. He had a Bluetooth in his ear so that he could talk to her hands free just in case their conversation got a little more… Interesting.

"Well," he'd deepened his voice, "that's exactly why I'm calling."

"So, you are coming to see me?" her voice shot up a pitch higher and he was sure she was going to start squealing.

"I'm scheduled to do a tour in the city in two weeks and I thought that maybe…" he lay there letting that last word just hang in the air.

Elise began squealing and screaming like a teenager, and he could almost imagine her kicking up her feet and stomping on her bed. He'd already asked what she was wearing and knew she was laying there in a satiny thong and a t-shirt that was cut at the midriff. In his mind he could see her breasts bouncing upon her chest and her legs flying about and it excited him beyond words. They'd not seen each other in over three months since he'd first met her at his book signing, and he'd been working on getting a book tour set up that would put them together even if it was for just one night.

"Are you just a little excited?" He teased her.

"Nah," was her quick return. "I think I may have a date that night."

"Well shit," Graylin was trying not to laugh, "that will work out perfectly. Your date can meet my side chick and maybe the four of us can go off and have a little swat and play."

"I am so going to kick your ass when I see you," Elise was laughing as hard as he was. "You do know that I am bi-sexual… right?"

Graylin sat up choking on the cigar and listening to her laugh at him. It was a good thing for the Bluetooth or else he'd have dropped a phone as well as his drink and he'd have spit the cigar across the room. Instantly his thoughts were of her beautiful face trapped between the legs of some faceless woman while he was behind her not only watching but participating in the fun.

"What the fuck did you just say?" he was trying to cough up the smoke still trapped in his lungs.

"You heard me," Elise was still laughing. "What? Do you think you could handle two women at once, Big Daddy?"

"Keep playing," Graylin warned. "You keep playing."

"Who says that I am, Baby?" her voice was low and sexy. "Maybe I want to feed another woman to you just to see how hungry you really are."

"You're a fucking tease, Elise," Graylin was chuckling. He'd dropped the cigar into the ashtray laying on the nightstand and sipped at his brandy before placing that glass on the table as well. His right hand was lightly rubbing against his thigh and he could feel his blood rushing towards his no longer dormant dick.

"Are you thinking about it?" Elise was in full teasing mode now and her voice was thick and heavy. "Do you see me stretched out between her spread thighs?"

"Hell yea," Graylin was sliding his hand against his lengthening shaft. "I can see you licking at her wet thighs but not going near her pussy, but she's already begging you to taste her."

"Mmmm," she was breathing heavy into the phone. "Can you see her hand on the back of my head trying to push me where she wants me? I'm not letting her have her way and I'm teasing and nibbling at her inner thighs. I can already hear her moaning."

"Yea," Graylin reciprocated. "Moaning and begging you for more and as you're taking care of her I'm staring at your sexy ass. Can you feel my tongue?"

Elise moaned out and Graylin could see her laying there with her legs spread and her fingers gently touching and teasing between her spread thighs. He could see her moving her fingers around the small piece of material and the sound her releasing that small bit of pent up air from her lungs let him know that her fingers had found what they were seeking. Her moans deepened, and he knew she was grinding that tight ass of her down into the bed as her fingers gently spread her moist lips open.

"That tongue feels so good, Daddy," her voice was a little high. "Don't stop... right there."

"Slowly sliding my tongue against the inside of your thighs and then across the wet lips of your pussy," Graylin was repaying the tease. "Spreading those lips of yours open and sucking down on your clit teasing it with the tip of my tongue before sliding back and pushing my tongue inside. Can you feel it, Baby?"

"God yes, you nasty motherfucking," she hissed out and he could tell that she was pushing her fingers slowly in and out of her pussy. Her voice was a little muffled and he knew she had her phone trapped between her ear and shoulder to keep it in place while she took care of business. "More… please, more."

"Damn, I can feel your sweet juices sliding along my tongue," Graylin was slowly stroking his length through his briefs. "Pushing in deep, slow fucking your pussy with this long, ass tongue as my chin bumps against your clit. Dragging my tongue out and up and against your tight little asshole."

"Oh, god, Graylin," she took a deep breath, "I so want you to do that. I'm so close, Baby, so fucking close. My clit hurts it's so fucking hard."

"I want to hear you cum for me, Elise," Graylin said thickly.

"Yes, Baby," she whispered into the phone. "Yes, make me cum… please."

■■■■

With the ringing of the alarm clock next to his bed, Graylin groaned at the incessant pounding on his room door. He pulled his tired body from the bed and reached for the wondrously soft bathrobe he'd draped across the foot of the bed after his shower last night. He stood stretching for a moment hoping that whatever was so urgent to require a beating at his door didn't take long because he wasn't dressed for visitors and had plans for sleeping in at least until noon. Pulling on the legs of his boxer briefs from being bunched up on his legs; he slipped on the robe's matching slippers at the edge of the bed before trudging towards the door… aggravated.

"Alright, damn," he spat out. "I'm coming… I'm coming, keep your goddamn panties on."

Pulling the door open he stared down at Aura as she held out a cup of coffee. He glared for a moment before accepting the cup and stepping aside and allowing her to walk in. Before he could stop his eyes wondered down her body and locked on the wiggling of her ass wrapped away behind that tight dress as she walked over to the sofa and sat down. He couldn't resist licking his lips at the thoughts he knew he shouldn't be having about her, but his overactive mind was already dwelling on.

"Why are you here so goddamn early?" he cleared his throat and closed the door. "I thought I told you last night that I didn't want to be disturbed this morning."

"You forgot, didn't you?" she cocked an eyebrow as she looked him in the eyes.

"Forgot... what?"

Huffing, Aura kicked off her shoes before tucking one leg under her butt. She ran her fingers through her short red hair before taking a big sip from her own cup of coffee. She knew it wasn't good to make him wait, but he deserved it this time after all that she'd put into him getting this on-air radio interview. Her green eyes stared out at him over the top of her cup waiting for some kind of recollection of their phone conversation to come back to him.

"The radio interview, Graylin," her disappointment was obvious. "It's been planned for over two weeks, so there's no pretending that you didn't know about it. I even put in your tablet and phone calendars just so that you wouldn't forget, and I reminded your ass last night on the telephone."

"Shit; in my defense, I was drinking last night so a lot of shit I said is really fucking foggy right now." Graylin cursed again before taking his first sip of the hot coffee and almost tossed the cup the moment the hot liquid burned his tongue. He stood in the middle of the room fuming because he'd actually forgotten about the interview. He wanted to kick Aura out because he wanted to sleep, but that was no longer an option.

Aura had had her fair share of dreams about Graylin Cross, but today was beyond anything that her imagination could have ever created. It was obvious that it had slipped his mind that he had on was his underwear under his robe, but his slip was her definitely entertaining for her. She sat on the sofa trying not to look obvious watching him pacing the floor. Each step across the plush carpeting and his robe flopped open at the waist exposing his dick pressed against the thin material of his boxers. She was biting on her bottom lip, and Graylin was paying no attention to her during his irate episode of ranting and raving. He was stomping his feet causing that lump in his shorts to slowly go from just laying flaccid to erect stretching down his thigh. Her imagination had given him an impressive tool, but seeing it growing had given her a new respect for what he normally kept hidden away in his pants.

Concentration on the man's tirade was next to impossible, and her body was already reacting. She was flexing her thigh muscles trying to clench and squelch the fire that was smoldering but that wasn't helping in the least. She'd placed her cup on the coffee table to keep from spilling it onto the floor as her eyes locked in on his growing member and her mind was going through a number of things that she'd love to do to him right at this moment.

"You need to calm down, Graylin," her voice trembled just a bit as she pulled her eyes from his crotch towards those... brown... eyes.

FUCK, she thought as he stared across the room at her. "Please, come sit down. The interview isn't until later today, but I knew if I didn't come over now you would have forgotten and just slept the day away."

"I've been on the road for almost two months straight, Aura," Graylin took a deep breath and moved over towards the sofa. "I think that you and Mishelle are trying to fucking kill me. I need some goddamn rest, and that was the part of my plan for most of today."

"Do you know how well the book sales are doing, Graylin?" Aura was still patting the sofa beside her for him to sit. "You're in the top 50 on the best sellers list and you're quickly running up the list."

"I understand that," he sounded like a scolded child as he stomped to the sofa, "but I need a fucking break."

The word fucking made her smile and tingle all over. She tried to swallow but coughed instead as he sat down, and the robe fell open from his legs. She had to fight her urges to look down because "it" was visibly outlined through his boxer briefs, and her instincts was to just reach out and …

"Are you listening to me, Aura?"

"Uh," she could feel his eyes on her as she turned her head away from his leg and tried to look up into her eyes. "Yes, Graylin, I'm listening, and I do understand. We just have this one interview and then two more stops and I promise we'll try to find a way to give you a good month off."

"Damn," he crossed his legs and dropped his head back on to sofa. "What time is the interview?"

Looking down at her watch and cutting her eyes over to look at his dick, Aura took a deep breath before answering, "We have to be there by 2:30, but the interview starts at around 3:15. We have a little time for you to, um, rest it's only 7:30."

"Shit," Graylin shook his head against the back of the sofa, "7:30, Aura… you fuckin' woke my ass up this early for some shit that ain't until this afternoon? You're a real piece of work."

"I know you, Big Boy," she giggled trying to keep her eyes on his face. "I know for a fact that if I don't get your procrastinating ass going early you'd miss everything. It's not done to be mean, Darry, it's done to maintain your status,"

"You know I hate it when you call me 'Darry'…" he was grinning as he sat up and glanced over at the beautiful woman beside him.

For the first time in a long time Graylin found himself paying attention to the woman sitting next to him. There'd been several close calls between them, and he'd always held out because he didn't want to mix his business with their moment of pleasure. He watched as her gorgeous, cat green eyes dropped from his eyes down towards his lap and he realized that his dick was pretty much on display for her to see. He watched as her breasts rose and fell quickly and her nipples had hardened trying to pierce through her dress. Her fingers were scratching at her thigh like she was trying to make a decision, but she was holding back as much as he was.

Reaching out, Graylin took her hand and moved it to his thigh. Her eyes came up to his and he could see a need there that he hadn't seen in any woman in a long time. Her fingers were gently stroking his bare leg and he could hear her breathing hard through pursed lips. He released her and waited for her to make her next move.

Aura closed her eyes and swallowed, for months she'd been having a reoccurring dream of Graylin fucking her into oblivion. She would wake up and her naked body would be covered in sweat and she'd be breathing, no she would be panting like she'd just experienced the orgasm of a lifetime. Her body would be shaking, and her thigh muscles would be jumping, and the bed beneath her ass would be soaked... like she'd just had the most intense orgasm of her life. She licked her lips as her fingers inched towards his swollen dick.

"I've wanted this for a long time," her breathing was heavy. "I know I; we shouldn't do this, but goddamn I think you're so fucking sexy."

"If we do this..." Graylin stopped her hand before her fingers touched his dick. "If we do this, Aura, nothing between us can change. Are you sure you can do this?"

"Yes," Aura quickly lied.

"Aura?" He reached over tucking his finger under her chin and lifting her head to stare into her eyes. "No strings... there can be no strings, and you have to promise."

Aura wrapped her fingers around the pulsating shaft and her mouth watered. She squirmed and pushed her ass down into the sofa as her fingers eased under the leg of his shorts and slid down his length. She tugged him free as her hand grazed along his skin until it was stopped by his public hairs and then slowly back up unto they butted the rim of his mushroomed head. Looking up her glazed stare tried to make contact with his eyes, but they were closed letting her know that he was already enjoying the stroking of her hand.

"I promise, Baby," she moaned as she shifted on the sofa and leaned forward to wrap her soft lips around his head.

"Goddamn," Graylin groaned as the wet heat of her mouth slowly drew him in and her hand continued to slip and slide along his fully hardened length. He'd imagined what she could do with her pretty mouth, but even as a writer, his imagination had failed him. Her teeth lightly scratched his sensitive flesh each time she'd pull her head back, and he could hear her attempting to swallow each time he stabs at the back of her throat. Her mouth was unlike anything he'd ever dealt with and her tongue was like the serpent from hell sent to torture him in ways he'd only had nightmares about.

Aura felt the floodgates in her mouth open and she drooled and slurped at the vibrating slab of thickness pressing against her tongue. Graylin was not to be denied his pleasure and he was thrusting his hips up each time she dropped her head and the swollen tip was demanding to entrance into her throat. She was breathing heavily through her nose because her lips refused to release her treat and she was determined to make him take back those words about the strings. His fingers had finally made it to her hair; he'd taken over and was gently thrusting into her welcoming mouth.

More, she kept repeating in her head as her nose flared. *More,* she kept chanting as his thrusts grew harder and more demanding. *More, god, please harder.*

Graylin had a firm hold of her hair as he stood up from the sofa. His robe fell open at the waist and her hands slide in along his thighs digging her nails into the back of his legs just below his ass. Reaching up, she tugged at the waistband of his boxer briefs dragging them down and only releasing his dick enough to pull the fabric out of her way before sucking him back between her lips. His hips were on automatic and he was thrusting forward as deep as her mouth would allow before pulling back as her throat willingly accepted the beating she was receiving. Graylin could hear her choking and smiled the moment he looked down and she was staring up at him with her make-up raccooned around her eyes and streaming down her face.

"Fucking beautiful," he slowly pulled back until the head was trapped behind her teeth; he pushed forward watching her cheeks balloon out and groaned out as her throat contracted trying to draw in deeper. "Suck it, Baby, let me see you work that cock."

Aura felt like her head was in the clouds. Her body felt like it was vibrating, and her brain was melting as this man that she'd been dreaming about was standing over her driving his cock into her throat and telling her that he wanted her. Her puss had been on a low simmer was now on a full boil and trapped away beneath her dress while she was on her knees. His strokes were long and hard each punctuated with him going deeper into her gullet causing her to choke and hyperventilate.

"Swallow it whole," Graylin could fell his toes curling into the carpet. He was trying not to scream, but it had been a while since a woman had given him head, and even longer since the last time it was anywhere near this goddamn good. She had her tongue swirling around the head each time he pulled back, and her throat was doing this crazy contracting thing on the head every time he pushed forward. He grunted at the light scratching of her nails on his balls, and he curled his fingers as best he could in her short hair as he thoroughly fucked her face.

"Get your ass up here," he'd pulled back grinning as her lips made this wet slurping/popping sound.

"But I want more," she whined as she was pulled to her feet. Her breathing was ragged as she adjusted back to breathing out of her mouth than through her nose. Her skin felt red, flushed, and on fire as Graylin pulled her face to his and their lips met in a kiss that weakened her knees. Her body fell into his arms and he kept her from falling and her arms had found the strength to move up his body to lock her fingers behind his head. Once again, she was trying to breathe through her nose; the kiss intensified, and she felt like she was burning from the inside out.

"Oh my god," she pulled back from his hungry mouth and sucked in a deep breath that barely calmed the flames in her lungs. "Wait... please gimme a second to catch my breath."

"Take your time," he'd spun her around and the sound of his voice in her ear made her shiver all over. His fingers were pulling down the zipper on her dress and easing the cloth from her body as she stiffened. Her breathing stopped. Her eyes closed. Aura swallowed trying to assure her mind that all of this was truly happening.

Graylin leaned into her neck and breathed in the delicious scent of her perfume and the sweet smell of the heat imitating from her skin. Her body trembled at the touch of his tongue sliding from her clavicle and up the side of her neck to her earlobe. She was pushing that tight, little ass of hers back against him and grinding keeping him good and hard. She was going to be more than he'd ever dreamed of in the last couple of years they'd been working together.

He slid his fingertips lightly down the sides of her arms, she hadn't worn a bra and her nipples just seemed to be anticipating his touch; he was gazing over her shoulders watching them harden as he drug his fingers up the sides of her breasts.

"You're killing me, Darry," she hissed through her teeth the moment he pinched and pulled at her very sensitive nipples. Most men she'd move their hands away and on to another part of her needy body, but she knew she wouldn't be able to deny him any part of her.

"I've been fighting this, Aura," his voice melted over her as he fondled and teased her breasts. "I've wanted to taste you for a long time, but I just wouldn't let myself."

"I know," her voice was barely audible. "But now?"

His fingers were pushing down on the thong she'd decided to wear. Her pussy was so hot that she could smell her need. Her panties were rolling past her hips and down thighs; Graylin was kneeling behind her and she almost screamed the moment his tongue slipped between her asscheeks. She stepped out of the thongs and he tossed the aside. His hand pushing at the small of her back quickly let her know that she was to lean forward, and the moment she did every nerve in her body exploded.

"Oh... My... Fucking... Lord." Aura felt like every inch of her shook violently as her first orgasm rocked her body. Her thighs tightened, and her ass clenched around his face as she pushed back trying to ride the length of his tongue torturing her unlike any man ever had. She could hear her voice chanting and begging for more as she kept telling him that she was cumming again that very second he struck her clit. Her knees buckled, but he had his arms wrapped around her holding her firm to his face.

"Fucking delicious," she could hear his voice from between her vibrating thighs, "and this is just the start."

Chapter 4: The Hot Seat

"I want to know what the hell's going on," Graylin demanded the moment the room door opened. He'd enough time to slow down and think; now he wanted answers.

"That's a good question, Mr. Cross," Detective Marcum slipped back into the interrogation room and took his seat. "I've sent a car to pick your wife..."

"Ex... wife" Graylin corrected. "She's my ex-wife. For almost three years now."

"That being said," Marcum continued, "we have a car going to pick her up."

"I doubt she'll be there, but that doesn't answer my question."

"True enough," Marcum sat back as Graylin sat down. "I didn't know about the restraining order and I'm having that pulled now as well. We're trying to get all of our ducks in a row here and unfortunately that puts you right in the middle of things."

"No shit," Graylin shook his head. "Did she really say that I did that to her?"

Graylin felt his eyes drawn back to the pictures of Elise. His stomach tuned at the sight. He'd written about things like he was gazing at, but he'd never actually see it was disturbing. How could anyone just beat another person like that, and not feel anything? The longer he studied the pictures the more he began to see Elise in his head begging and pleading for her life, and again his stomach turned.

"Could you please put those away?" He finally found the words as Marcum sat across from him just watching. "Please, Detective, I can't deal with seeing her like that. Please?"

"I must say that I'm kind of surprised here, Mr. Cross." Marcum gathered up the pictures and slid them away inside of their folder.

"Oh, yeah?" The sarcasm was blatant, as he wiped the back of his hand across his brow. "And why's that, Detective Marcum?"

"Well I know that you're this hotshot writer and that your Forte of late is murder thrillers and stories about serial killers."

"Okay... and?"

"Why would a few pictures make a man like you, in the business that you're in, queasy? You write about this kind of stuff and sometimes it's a lot worse."

"Yes, I write about it, I research it and I study it..." Graylin felt like the room was crowding in on him. His chest hurt like it was hard to breathe, and the room felt like it was spinning around him. He tried gulping in deeper breaths of air, but his throat was constricted like it was blocked.

"Cross?" Marcum was leaping from his seat as he watched the man struggling. He was screaming for a medic to the people that he knew were on the other side of the mirrored glass that had been behind him. Everything was moving in slow motion and all he could think of was catching the collapsing man before his head hit the metal table. Marcum cursed as he almost tripped.

"Get someone in here now goddammit."

Graylin felt like his heart was trying to beat its way out of his chest with a sledgehammer. His lungs were starving to breathe in any kind of air, but his throat refused to open up. He was wheezing through his nose and pursed lips. His eyes were rolling back into his, and his legs buckled tossing him forward towards the table. He wanted to scream but couldn't drag any sounds from his throat. He wanted to stop his fall, but his arms refused to move, and all he could do was watch in horrified silence.

"What the hell just happened?" Marcum was gently laying the unconscious Cross on the floor as his captain and the med staff rushed in.

"Beats the shit out of me, Cap," Marcum stood wiping the sweat from his brow as he stepped away from the now kneeling paramedics. Captain Enessa Rowlings stood staring at him with her hands on her slender hips. He had a lot of respect for this woman, he'd come up through the ranks together, and she was one of the first black women to captain a precinct in this district. The moment that she got her stripes she'd come looking for to head up her detective department.

Shit," the word didn't sound right coming from her, but he understood. "Was it the pictures?"

"From what I can tell, Nessa," he was leaning in so that the conversation was just between them, "there's something really odd going on here. I mean this man writes about this kind of stuff and yet he passes out like a first-time dad in the delivery room. But, the woman's report was so goddamn convincing."

"I want her back in here now," Rowlings demanded knowing that Marcum was already on top of things. The one thing that she knew about her top detective, he could smell bullshit from miles away.

"Yea, I got Abraham on it right now, as well as the restraining order that the leads forgot to mention..."

"I'll take care of those two in a bit," Rowlings looked aggravated as she looked around Marcum hoping that their lead suspect was no long passed out on her interrogation room floor. "What are your thoughts on the other women?"

Marcum ran his fingers through his thinning hair. He'd had every intention on grilling Cross on the files of the other three women, but with this development... Graylin Cross couldn't be his man.

"To be honest," he took a deep breath and shoved his hands into the pockets of his slacks, "I don't think Cross has the balls to off those women."

"So how are they all connected to Cross?"

"That's the million-dollar question," Marcum was shaking his head. "I have more questions than answers, Cap, but we need to him answer a few I'm sure."

"Captain... Marcum," Abraham was speed walking towards them waving a fist full of papers.

"What did you find?" Captain Rowling waved her forward.

"The R.O. was issued about six months ago," Abraham held out the papers. "Guess how many times Mr. Cross has called in to the police."

Rowlings stares at the report for several long moments before passing them on to Marcum. Her forehead was furrowed as she stood there trying to let everything register. In those six months Graylin had called for police and fire assistance a total of twenty-four times.

"That's like four times a month," Marcum replied flipping through the pages. "That's ridiculous, Abraham, I need you to go through his schedule, I want to know how it correlates to each death. We already know that he was out of town when the ex-wife was beaten"

"On it," she off and running down the hall.

"I'm going to get a CSI team back over to their houses," Rowlings was walking off talking over her shoulder, "I want both torn apart if need be, something was missed, and I want to know what. I refuse to have this department played for fools."

"I'll get back on him yet moment he's cleared to speak."

"Keep me informed."

She was a hard-nosed woman and accepted absolutely no nonsense from anyone, but most especially her officers. Rowlings ran a tough ship but she was fair, and that's what Marcum respected the most about her. He noticed that shortly after taking the captain's position, she kept her dark, wavy hair tied back off of her face and her suits were a bit looser than they'd been when she worked homicide as his partner. He smirked a bit recalling the way her pants hugged her hips and the fact that she didn't mind sharing a little cleavage.

Damn, I miss the good old days, he shook his head as he turned to walk back into the interrogation room.

"Mr. Cross?"

Graylin was sitting in the chair with his arms on the table, his shoulders slumped and his head down. Upon first glance Marcum thought that the man was crying, but as Graylin rose up to look across the room, Marcum could see now that he was still trying to control his breathing.

"You gave us a bit of a scare."

"The paramedics said it wasn't a heart attack," he shrugged his shoulders. "It was a severe panic attack. First time that's ever happened... that bad."

"You've been through quite a lot in the last few hours." Marcum sounded apologetic as he took his seat across the table. "The problem this isn't the end of it."

"Meaning?" Graylin stared at the detective trying to remain calm.

"I have more questions, Mr. Cross, questions concerning a few other women that you may have been involved with. Look, I'll be honest with you, there's some crazy shit happening and it's all pointing at you."

"I... I don't understand," Graylin stuttered a puzzled look on his face. "What the hell's going on?"

"If I had to put my finger," Marcum leaned over the table lowering his voice, "I'd say one of two things is happening here. Either you're really good and this is just an act to throw us off of you as our primary subject in an ongoing investigation, or you've pissed off someone very smart whose implicating you some shit that can get you sent away for a very long time."

Marcum sat back watching. It was a tactic he'd used a number of times just to observe the responses. The guilty generally answered too quickly, too defensively and that would always explain a lot to him. There have been those few sociopaths that would give him that smug, smartass smile that would let him know that they thought him too stupid to catch them. But, there were those like Graylin Cross who would sit thinking, letting his words roll around a few dozen times in their heads while staring at him like a deer caught in the headlights of a car.

Those were the ones that could fall... either way.

"Are you telling me that," Graylin sat back trying to truly grasp what he was being told. His mind spun and the headache he'd been suffering intensified. His stomach was churning again, and his mouth was dry and tacky making talking hard. He'd written about shit like this; an innocent man being interrogated for mur...

"Wait... wait," he was reeling," someone's de--, dead? Are you saying that I'm a suspect for mu--, for murder?"

Marcum sat quietly watching the different expressions Cross' face contorted through as the seriousness of his current situation hit him like a ton of bricks. This could all be a part of the play to maintain his "innocence", but there was something very genuine in the younger man's responses. Folding his arms across his chest, Marcum waited, trying to decide his next course of questions. It would most likely take a while for Abraham to compile the information he'd requested that she look into, but that shouldn't leave him without an avenue or two to test...

But he was actually stomped.

I'm not a killer. Graylin could hear the words but they weren't from his mouth. His tongue was too heavy to lift, and his mouth to dry for him to articulate. He was looking around without moving his head testing theories of escape in his head, and all of them were failing. His hands were balled so tight that his knuckles whitened, and he could feel the nails digging into the palms.

You have to calm down, Cross. This was his voice of reason, but his reasoning was shut down and he was in full panic mode. *I've written this time and again, and how many times has my protagonist just sunk deeper and deeper into shit? I'm being railroaded, set the fuck up for some bullshit.*

The man's face was flashing different emotions all running into the other as Marcum sat still silent. It was all a part of his own play just to see how he could wrangle the responses he needed to slam a case close. He could see Cross' lips moving, there were no vocal words, but he'd studied lip reading through a detective training course with the FBI some years ago and it always came in handy. Graylin was arguing with himself and if this hadn't been something serious, he would have found this entire act amusing.

"Mr. Cross?" he'd cleared his throat attempting to get his suspect's attention. "Mr. Cross, we have to continue. Are you ready to continue?"

"Are you charging me with some kind of crime, Detective?" Graylin was heated and the anger tinged his voice. "If you're saying that you think I... killed someone, then I'm not saying shit else."

"We're not charging you," Marcum sat back staring into the writer's eyes and seeing the one thing he was trying to avoid... him shutting down and lawyering up. "We just want to ask a few more questions before..."

"Before... what?" All of his years of researching investigations and interrogations raced through his head. "Before you decide to read me my rights on suspicion?"

"We merely wish to talk," Marcum was trying in vain to diffuse situation. "There's something going on here and whatever it is you're in the middle of it. It would be in your..."

"Best interest to cooperate," Graylin finished the detective's sentence. "You can finish talking to me when I can have my lawyer present."

Graylin sat back in the seat with his arms folded across his chest. His face now was a stone mask and eyes were cold. He was done with the games, and the only thing that he wanted to do was get the fuck up out of this place. In his mind he began going through the pictures of Elise beaten.

Shit, a million thoughts raced through his head, *who does she know that will beat her like that? Better still, why blame me?*

■■■■

"You're not supposed to be here, Elise?" Graylin was livid seeing his ex-wife standing at his door.

"We need to talk, Graylin," Elise had her fists pressed against her hips. Her long, dark hair was pulled up into a ponytail away from her face allowing for her eyes and expressions.

"You know that we don't talk," Graylin frowned trying not to stare into her eyes. "All we do is argue and fuck, and I'm not in the mood for either with you. You need to go."

"I'm not leaving until we talk," her brow furrowed.

"I'm closing my door..." he began his threat.

"And I'll stand here beating on your goddamn door," she interrupted. "You're going to hear me out."

"This is why I got the restraining order," Graylin stepped out of his house keeping the door cracked. "This shit right here is why you're my ex-wife."

"We're still married, you son-of-a-bitch," her tone sent a chill up and down his spine, and the look in her eyes scared the shit out of him. "You really think that you can just throw me away that easily, Graylin? What? Am I just some trash to be tossed aside?"

"Keep your voice down," he hissed through his teeth as her voice rose with each word.

"Why? You got that little bitch in there?"

It was Graylin turn to laugh as his ex-wife stared at him. Her expressions alone made his inside joke that much funnier that he almost stumbled down the short flight of stairs at his door. This was something about her he was well used to; throughout their marriage she'd made a point of trying to keep him under thumb and he'd allowed it. A number of times he'd found some application on his cell phone that could GPS wherever he was; she'd put Spyware on his laptop just to see what he was doing and websites he'd been on; and she'd hacked a few of his email accounts just to read his mail. His laughter was hurting his stomach.

"What's so fucking funny, Graylin?" She was aggravated, and he knew she was on the verge of exploding.

"You really need to go, Elise," Graylin was wiping his eyes and trying to stop the laughing, but she was making it hard on him. "I've spent way too much time trying to tell you that you can't catch me in shit. The red head... you fucking know her, you've met her, Elise, she's my publicist Aura. I love it, I mean I really do... you need to tell who ever it is you got watching me to stop or if they're going to report shit to you know what the fuck they're talking about."

"Who do you think you're fooling, Graylin, I know that you're fucking her," Elise was yelling as she got up in his face.

"No, Baby, you just think you know," he was no longer laughing but the mirth was still shining in his eyes. "You've invested so much time trying to catch me in shit and wasted all of my time trying to love you. I'm so done with your ass. I'm through with all of this."

"This what?" Elise was beyond pissed and paced the small space trying not to swing out at him. He was staring at her like she was trash, and she couldn't figure out why. She wanted to scream. She wanted to hit something. She wanted someone to... Him.

She had wanted him to hit... her.

"I hate you." She was breathing heavy and her fingernails were biting into her palm. Tears were streaming from her eyes and she feel his eyes on her. She hated crying, especially over him because he always made her feel as if he didn't care. "I fucking hate you, you sorry son-of-a-bitch."

"You can hate me all you want," Graylin had his arms folded across his chest watching her little show. He'd noticed that a few of his neighbors had come out and were watching the spectacle that was once his wife. "You need to leave my house, Elise or I'm calling the cops."

"You think this is how this is going to end? You really believe..."

"What I believe is that I'm tired if this shit, right here," Graylin was leaning forward waving his hand between them. "Enough is enough, Elise. You hate me, so leave me the fuck alone. It's really that simple... you go your way and I'll go mine."

"No..." Elise swallowed hard trying to choke back what she could feel coming. Her pain was burning her up from the inside and he was the cause. "No, Graylin, no..."

"Good bye, Elise," he stepped back into his house. "This shit is over. Don't ever come back here or I will call the police... understand."

"Think what you want, Graylin," Elise was slowly backing down the stairs, "but we're not through; not by a long shot, Baby. You'll see."

"Good bye, Elise." He closed his door and locked it. A deep sigh slipped from his lips as he slumped back against the thick wood just hoping she would leave.

"You're going to be sorry, Motherfucker!" He could hear her screaming from outside. "You'll regret this, Graylin, you're gonna regret all of this."

"Please just go away," he repeated over and over until it was finally quiet.

"I take it that the crazy bitch was outside?" Aura stood in front of him in one of his dress shirts; she looked gorgeous, but all he wanted to do was laugh again. Elise would be pissed beyond words if she could see the "red head bitch" right now.

"Yea," his smile was huge, "it was her looking for you.

Chapter 5: Meeting Again

"We've lost him," Marcum said disgustedly as Captain Rowlings and Abraham walked up.

"What happened?" Rowlings demanded.

Marcum quickly gave them the Clift notes version of the last hour he'd spent with Graylin Cross. His hands were stuffed into his pants to keep him from flailing them about madly. He was beyond pissed that he'd somehow blown this opportunity with his best suited suspect because the man had clammed up.

"Dammit," Rowlings shook her head. She knew how crafty and how skilled Marcum was in the interrogation room, but now they had nothing to go on. And, if Cross hadn't beat his wife, was he responsible for the other three women. "Where do we stand on the murders?"

"He was our best suspect," Marcum dropped bluntly. "Until just a bit ago, I was sure he'd beat the shit out of his wife. Now we're back at square one. I want to get all of our files together and go through them all with a fine-tooth comb."

"Well I can confirm that Cross was out of town," Abraham passed Marcum the paper she'd been holding. "Witnesses can have him in place just moments before the 9-1-1 call was placed making it impossible to anywhere near town. There's also a clear shot of him from an airport security camera about an hour before being picked up."

"Excellent," Marcum pushed his hand through hair. "This whole investigation is up in smoke. Any more good news?"

"I've sent the CSI unit back out to the scene since we're bringing in the ex-wife," Rowlings stated. "And I've told them not to return until they have something concrete that we can use."

"I don't know what good that will do."

"Why do you say that, Sarg?" Abraham was looking back and forth between her two superiors.

"The more I think on this," Marcum began and then looked back at the door to the interrogation room, "I'm beginning to think that Ms. Mannsen may have done this to herself or had someone do it to her. To me that would put her in the range of being damn near sociopathic. If she's willing to go through all of that, who's to say what else she's capable of."

"Are you thinking that she may have had those women killed?" Rowlings stared at her senior detective as the thoughts of what he was suggesting flashed through her own process.

Marcum shrugged his shoulders, but the fact that he'd sat there watching Graylin Cross as he began trying to sort things out had him pretty convinced that the man was not the guilty party. From the beginning of this investigation when they received the LynMarie Craig case he'd been building up everything against this man after he'd found out about their affair. His initial thoughts were that Cross had been rebuffed by the woman and to teach her a lesson… he'd beaten her to death. That train of thought was cemented the moment the second case of Sadè Jefferies was dropped on his desk and then Trinity Wheeling; all three women had been beaten to death.

"What if the profile was wrong because we were all profiling the previous three beatings as being done by a man?"

"Yes, basically a crime of passion; all of the women were beaten in their faces like 'he' didn't want to see them. Then they were all stabbed numerous times between the abdomen and the chest. The unsub was angry."

"Yes," Marcum was nodding his head. "Yes, very angry, but what if the passion part was more to who the women were and not who they'd been with. All of them were lovers of Graylin Cross, but Jefferies was before his marriage because she was the mother of his one child; Wheeling was a woman he was with during the time just after they'd separated; and Craig was someone he'd just recently been seeing."

"We need to find out how she found out about these women," Rowlings mind was going a mile a minute. She was angry because her department was almost played by this very conniving woman. She'd come to expect great and precise things from her officers and at this moment Marcum was proving why he was the best man on her team. "We need to get on top of this, Erick, before the Commissioner and the Mayor start chewing into my ass. We're completely behind the eight ball because we've been concentrating our energies in the wrong direction."

"She'll be here in moments, Captain," Abraham looked around expecting to see a couple of her fellow officers to be escorting her in, "how do we proceed with our interrogation of her?"

"Damn good question," her sigh was deep and heavy. "Erick?"

"I think we don't let her in on the fact that our prime suspect has changed from her ex," Marcum was already thinking of how to move forward. "The moment she thinks that we're looking at her I fear she will escalate more than she has already."

"Agreed." Rowlings began walking away.

"What about Cross, Captain?" Abraham asked the question everyone needed and answer to. "Do we continue to hold him or do we…"

"Let him go," Rowlings answered without looking back. We don't have enough to hold him on and he's already asking for his lawyer. Let's take that option off of the table. Just apologize but remind him not to leave the city."

■■■

"So, how's the steak?" Graylin bit down another fork full of his own perfectly cooked porterhouse.

"This is delicious," Elise was grinning from ear to ear. "How did you find out about this place? I live here and didn't know this existed."

"It was pretty simple, I had my publicist look up steak houses and this one came highly recommended and it was not easy to get in to. Somehow Aura knew someone who could get us a reservation for tonight even though there were no openings for a good month and a half."

"And there you have it," Elise was giggling, "the red head is more than just a pretty face that you keep around."

"She's a damn good friend," Graylin smiled. "We've been working together for a couple of years now, and I have to admit… I never knew what good having a publicist was until Mishelle put her on my team."

Graylin had come into town with no other plans in mind other than taking this beautiful and patient woman out to dinner. They'd been talking over the phone for a little more than two months and he'd made promise after promise to go out and see her, but at each and every turn something would come up. He could no longer count the number of radio interviews and book signings he'd been on, but he knew one thing… he was tired and needed some time off.

"So," Elise drawing his attention back onto her, "two questions for you."

"Shoot…"

"Where are you staying and how long will you be here."

"A little place right off the highway named La Kiva Hotel," Graylin had to stop and think of the name for a second. "And, I'll be here for a few days. Why? Would you like to come stay with me?"

"Would you like for me to come stay with you, Graylin?"

Elise was staring at him over the rim of her glass. Her blues eyes just seemed to burn into his leaving him unable to really say much but in his mind the things that he was doing to her just may be considered illegal in most states. She was absolutely breath taking, and it was like he was looking at her for the first time all over again. The little black dress she was wearing seemed to be painted to her body leaving him unable to imagine anything short of trying to rip it off. Her slender feet were delicately decorated in a pair of four-inch stilettos that accentuated her calf muscles in ways he'd only written about; and her raven black hair was loose, flowing down to the middle of her back and there was this one piece that just fell perfectly over her left eye.

"You are absolutely beautiful," he finally managed to speak again.

"Thank you," she grinned. "But, you didn't answer my question."

"Amazing how you answered my question by directing the same damn question to me. I would love for you to stay with me while I'm here," his answered made her smile broadened, "but only if you would like to stay with me."

"I would love to stay with you, Mr. Cross," she giggled a little girly giggle that made him grin. She shivered the moment he reached across the table and touched her hand, and her eyes glazed over a bit making it hard to see him.

Her crush on Graylin Cross began a few years ago after she'd read his first book about a rogue vampire that had decided to go against his coven. She'd fallen in love with his words and the way that he was able to draw a reader into the worlds he'd created. He was such a beautiful man to her and she'd only seen his pictures. He wasn't one of those famous author types that would traipse around with one woman after the next glued to his arm at his side, and from a few interviews she'd read he was definitely a down-to-earth, southern man that she would love to meet.

Elise was staring at his lips. She'd taken almost every picture that she could find of him and had them blown up just so that she could cut out his lips. She had them on one of the walls in her room just so that she could stare at them any time she wanted to. She'd memorized them and had longed to just reach out and touch them. She licked her own lips as she watched him talking.

"I want you," she blurted out.

"Do you really?" he was teasing her and that never ceased exciting her.

"Yes," she was nodding, "I really want you… badly."

"I could pay the bill and we can get the hell up outta here."

"Please," she was sure she was begging, but she didn't care. Her body was on fire sitting across this slab of wood from him and if something was done soon she would explode. "Please, Graylin, get me out of here."

Raising a hand to garner the attention of their waitress, Graylin called the young lady over as he reached into his jacket to retrieve his wallet. "I need the bill please," he requested once the girl was in earshot. She smiled and walked back off to the register to calculate the final bill. He sat there trying not to be impatient while they waited for her return. With his credit card at the ready, he handed it to their waitress with the newly signed bill.

"You think we should stop for some wine and snacks for later?" he asked Elise as she stared at him.

"We can do anything… and I do mean anything that you want."

"Be careful," he winked.

"No, Baby, you be careful, or you'll find your hands full."

"I have big hands, Darlin'," his smile was full, "and I love having them full."

"Now who's being the tease?" She was standing as he walked around to hold her chair for her. She leaned forward just a bit so that he could get a quick look down the front of her dress leaving him wondering.

"I would definitely have to say that you're being the tease."

The moment the waitress returned Graylin accepted his card and he walked just slightly behind Elise enjoying the swing of her hips. He was immediately in love with the shape of her legs in those damn heels as each step made her ass bounce in a way that he was sure she was singing a song in her head. She had the body of a dancer and a track and field athlete, the muscles were toned and fit and moved like they were choreographed. It was damn good that his slacks were loose or everyone they walked by would be privy to the growth going on in that general area.

"Enjoying the view?"

"More than you'd think I would," he'd stepped up beside her and slid his hand down from the small of her back to palm her ass.

"So, brass," she leaned into his body as they left the restaurant into the cool of the night. She smiled as he pulled off his jacket and draped it over her shoulders. The walk to his rental was a short one and she was thankful because she was ready to get those heels off of her feet. Stepping up into the SUV and sinking into the soft leather she took a deep breath and smiled because the truck smelled just like his cologne. Leaning over she unlocked his door and waited for him to join her.

"Comfy?" he asked as she snuggled down into the seat. The music was a soft jazzy tuned that he turned down just, so it wasn't too loud.

"Very, but I can't wait."

"Wait for what?" he glanced at her for a second before pulling out into the traffic.

Elise didn't answer, but the look in her eyes told him everything that he needed to know. Her body was slowly gyrating against the seat and the door as she moved with the sounds of the horns playing through the speakers. Her eyes were closed, and she was lip syncing a silent song in her head. Even in the dark and the dancing shadows of being in the truck he was taking glances at a goddess, and she was coming home with him. His own Aphrodite and he was planning to make love to her nine ways to Sunday.

The drive across town was a quick one, it was simply amazing how loose the traffic was, and he was back at the hotel before they both had realized it. He parked close to close enough for her to get out quick and they were both running up the stairs to his room. The night was cool, there was a soft breeze that gently slipped through her hair as he stared at her leaning against the rail waiting for him to open up and invite her in.

Graylin hesitated. He turned and held out his hand to her and she quickly took it. He pulled her into his arms and held her tight as her ocean blue eyes allowed him to fall in and drown before he pressed his lips to hers for their very first kiss. Her lips were the softest that he'd ever touched, and they opened up to him immediately allowing his tongue entrance into her mouth. Her fingers were lightly scratching at the base of his neck as his hands slid down her back to grab her ass. She moaned into his mouth and it felt as if his entire body was melting.

"Take me inside, Baby," she'd pulled away from his mouth as was biting on his earlobe, "and… Take Me."

■■■■

"Mr. Cross," Marcum had come back into the room followed closely by his Amazon of a partner and the headache that had been building burst. Marcus looked up shaking his head.

"I've already told you, Detective Marcum, that I am fucking done. If you want to ask me any more goddamn questions you'd better get my attorney in here right now. If I'm not being charged with shit… I'm ready to get the fuck out of here."

"That's what I came in to tell you, Sir, on behalf of our entire department, I'd like to offer an apology for detaining you and to offer you a ride back to your home."

"I'm free to go?" Graylin was astounded that his demands had gotten him the response it had; shit, this worked better than it had in most of his stories. In the stories the demand for a lawyer would have been met with so much bullshit from the pressuring detectives that his character would be almost singing to whatever tune the cops played.

There had to be more to this than what was being offered, but he slowly stood and made his way towards the door. In the back of his mind he was waiting for the two cops to jump him the moment that he touched the door, slamming him to the floor and screaming out that he was trying to escape… but nothing happened. Marcum was standing with his hand on the knob as he approached.

"I know that we've given you a lot of shit to think about, Mr. Cross, but I must again apologize, and I have to ask you not to leave town without informing us. This investigation is still going on and we may need to ask you some more questions."

"I don't give a fuck what you may have to ask," he was irritated that the man was still blocking his way out of the small and confining room. "I just want to go home and wash the smell of this place from my body. Can you please move… Detective?"

"May I offer you a ride home, Sir?"

"I think I'll take a cab." Graylin reached down and moved the man's hand from the door knob and made his way out into the main room of the police precinct.

His step was a little unsure because he'd been sitting for a while and his foot had fallen asleep. He was angrier than words can describe because they'd pulled him from his home and dropped him into that small room and they'd accused him of things he'd only written about. He was completely confused because from the way things had been described to him Elise had blamed him for beating the shit out of her, and she knew that he'd never touch her like that. AND, to top things off, the cops had wanted to make him responsible for some other murders of women he had undoubtedly known.

Graylin had had some bad days in his life, but this day had to be at the top of the list. In moments he'd gone from almost being another "black" statistic and seeing the rest of his life from behind bars, to being someone that the cops needed to remain in town for more questioning. He stopped for a moment and took a deep breath trying to calm his nerves. He'd closed his eyes and threw his head back hoping that the slight massage to his temples would ease of the vice grip pain that his brain was suffering. As he opened his eyes, he had to blink them hard to make certain he was seeing… what he was seeing.

He knew that walk anywhere. The sway of those hips was unmistakable, and even in those large fitting sweatpants he could never miss the bounce of that ass. Dropping his hands from head his steps towards the woman just ahead of him was quick. Her raven dark hair was up high on her head in a flouncing around ponytail leaving the back of her neck clear for him to see the black and blue rings of bruises. His words caught in his throat and he tried to choke out her name, but the hands of Marcum and Abraham had finally caught up to him before he could reach out…

"E… Elise?" the words were more of a cry. "Dear God… Elise, is that?"

She turned, and his heart nearly stopped. Her beautiful, pale face was marred with more bruises than most boxers ended up with after a match. Her eyes were swollen and the left one nearly closed. The skin around the bruising looked painfully red and he could see that it had been bleeding. There were stitches at the corner of her mouth where it had been split open. The bruising on her neck was around on the front as well, and her cheeks were nearly twice their normal side.

"What the hell happened?" his eyes were blurred by the tears as he snatched away from the two cops and walked up to his ex-wife. He gently touched her face as she stared up at him before she was pulled into his arms. "Whoever did this to you… I swear, Baby, I swear I'm going to find them and I'm going to beat the living shit out of them. You have my word ok… you have my word."

Chapter 6: Frail Memories

(6 months before the arrest)

"Good evening, welcome to BayNews at ten... I'm Elene Danvers."

Graylin was a creature of habit, walking into his den he immediately switched on the television and was already ignoring it. As a writer, he needed the sounds to keep his mind concentrating on what he was about to get into; there were times he'd have the music cranked, other times it was the television, and then there were a lot of times it was both.

"How the hell can you write with the TV. and the music going?" Elise would often ask.

"Not really sure," he'd always answer with a shrug of his shoulders. "I've been this way for as long as I remember. It would aggravate my mom to no ends, but my pops seemed to understand."

"Why ever did I marry such a crazy man?" she teased.

"Well, because I'm cute, and funny, and because I am oh so creative."

Graylin shook his head trying to quickly move past the memory. Elise, a woman he'd dreamed of truly making a family with, had become a woman of his worst dreams. For almost seven years they'd spent more time arguing or not talking to one another more often than any of the good times. He actually had to stop and put in a lot of thought into any of the good times that they did have, and even those were usually short lived and quickly spoiled.

"Damn," he said it aloud just to hear his voice as he walked to his bar and fixed a nice stiff bourbon and went to his desk to begin working.

Sitting down, he glanced down at his cell and realized that he hadn't heard from Trinity in a few days. He scrolled through his call history and realized that the last time he'd actually talked to her in almost a week and it was completely unlike her to return his calls. He'd been getting worried, and a crazy part of him wanted to try to contact her husband just to check on her; he'd thought of pretending to be a business associate or something, but each time he'd go to make the call...

"She's ok, Cross," he told himself again and again. "Just keep calm, she's probably trying to work on her marriage and you cannot be a part of that equation."

The chair at his desk was one of those overstuffed leather chairs that he'd always imagined sitting in when he first started writing. The back reclined, and the base rocked which he utilized a lot when he was in his thinking mode or caught up in how he wanted a chapter to go. The chair was seriously comfortable, but today he just couldn't seem to enjoy sitting in it.

"Where the hell are you, Trinity?" he stared up at the television but wasn't really seeing anything. His mind was on her and the fact that she hadn't been in touch since they'd made plans to see each other again thanks to a radio interview and a huge book convention and signing tour that was beginning in Denver and he was a part of it from beginning to end.

A smile creased his lips as he thought of about the first time they'd finally met.

■■■

So, I'll be in Your area soon.
Trinity's words floated on his computer screen and he stopped everything. The words to the new book he'd been working on ceased and all he could do was stare. They'd been talking about meeting for months, and it had always seemed impossible; she lived in the mid-west and he was of course in the south, and their schedules were both ridiculous with both of them traveling all of the time. He glanced away for a second and drew in a deep breath and released slow as he focused on the calendar hanging on the wall beside his desk.
Hey, did I lose You? Did You see what I said?
"Play it cool, Graylin, play it cool."
Yes, I'm here, Darlin. So, you're coming this way, huh? When?
In two weeks. It was like he could hear the pause in her voice. *I want to see You... bad.*
How bad?
He was teasing her now because he loved getting her all worked up. Their conversations the last few weeks were becoming increasingly hotter, and the tension was obvious. And the need to finally meet was shared. He'd seen pictures, nothing provocative, but they were enough to pique his interests; he loved her eyes because they were this golden brown that just seemed hypnotic, and she had a smile that he couldn't wait to see up close and personal. They'd also been talking on the phone, and he wanted to see if that little cowgirl twang was real.
You already know how bad, Daddy.

She knew what strings to pull to get the responses she sought; even though she couldn't see him she knew exactly where his hand was, and he could imagine her smiling.

You're So bad, Girl... You know that?

But only for You, Daddy.

Yes, that's what you keep telling me. Where are you going to be staying?

You know I wouldn't lie to You...

I know, but I also know that he's there with you too.

The "he" was her husband and from the stories that she'd been telling him there was pretty much no love left between them, but to divorce him would create a big battle over the company and the money. She'd teased him several times when it came to her husband that it was cheaper to keep him but made more financial sense to just "get rid of him". Graylin would always get a shiver when she'd say that, but it would remind him of some of the characters that he'd created.

Graylin, you know he means nothing to me... right? I need You to understand that. I need for you to believe me.

It's not that I don't believe you... honestly, Trinity, I'm not sure where all of this is going with the two of us. When I look at the shit I'm going through and then you're there with what you're dealing with... I mean, is it good for us to even get into this right now?

Do You want me to stop? I can if that's what You want of me. I'll do whatever it is You want because I only want to make You happy in whatever way that I can.

He sat back in his chair letting it rock back and forth as he read and reread what she'd just typed. Again, it wasn't the first time she'd made that offer; in truth, she'd typed that or even said as much and as often as she had the inside joke about getting rid of him. Whenever he thought about her, he wanted to see her. He wanted to hear her voice and his day wasn't complete until they'd spoken on the phone. He'd had dreams of making love to her and hearing her cry out his name as her orgasm shook her entire body beneath him. Even now, sitting here contemplating tell her that they should stop, his body was excited at the thought of finally getting his hands on her.

Where are you going to be staying? His fingers were shaking as he typed out those few words and then he waited to see her reply.

I have a suite at the W Atlanta-Midtown that will have a beautiful view of the city and we'll have a sunken tub that we can share...how does that sound? Would You like the room number?

Of course, I would, he typed out quickly hoping that it would put a smile on her face.

So, does this mean that after all of this time we'll finally get to meet? You're not going to cancel out on me at the last minute... are you?

There will be no cancelling. I haven't been to ATL in a while. I'll get some signings set up there, so I can keep busy while you're taking care of your business.

That sounds like a plan.

Graylin sat there staring at the computer screen and in his mind, he was already texting Aura to get things in play in Atlanta so that he'd be all set up in the next two weeks. It was true that he hadn't been in a while, but the good thing about that was the last time he did a signing there it had gone over quite well. He'd been sitting on the bed and had to adjust the pillows at his back as he smiled at the screen and their conversation.

Picking his cell, he sat it down and turned back to his computer. *I'm not telling anyone anything... this way no one can disturb our time together... I'm just slipping out of town for a few days.*

Are you sure, Daddy? I know how your people can be, about like mine if I were to just disappear.

I'm positive... shit I need this time. Things with the ex-wife have been ridiculous and I just want some time to recharge.

LOL... I don't know if you'll be recharging if I get my way.

Graylin laughed as he read that last line. They'd been teasing each other unmercifully and even though they'd never sent each other any pictures beyond face and fully clothed ones, he had already seen her butt naked and kneeling at his feet a number of times.

We shall see, little girl...

You know I'm Yours to command, Daddy... I'll text You the room information the moment my people confirm it in the morning.

Good... I'll clear out my calendar and be at your door before you know it.

God, I cannot wait... he could imagine her sitting on her bed licking her lips most likely dressed in that Cowboys t-shirt she loved to wear. He could picture his hands running up the sides of her thighs moving under the edge of her shirt to her bare hips and then her waist and pulling her flat on the bed. His tongue slowly tracing his way over her knee as his hands move the shirt out of his way exposing her to his hungry eyes.

I'm tired, Daddy, may this girl go to bed?

"Damn," Graylin reached down and quickly adjusted his dick in the sweats he had on. "We're going to end up killing each other.

Yes, little girl, you may go to bed... but there will be no touching My pussy tonight. You lay there next to his snoring ass and have dreams of Me getting My hands on you very soon.

I so can't wait, Graylin. She rarely ever called him by his name, and her doing so right now brought out a huge smile on his face. He couldn't wait to finally see her either. He couldn't wait to taste her lips for the first time and to hear her moan. He couldn't wait to hear her voice beyond the muffle of the telephone. His dreams of making her scream out his name were about to come true.

Neither can I, Trinity. Rest well, Baby, and text Me in the morning. Always, sleep well, my Love.

The time passed quickly enough and Graylin had spent a lot of that time working on a new book and away from the signing circuit. He'd told Mishelle that he needed some time away from the crowds to get some major writing in, and amazingly enough... she had agreed. He was two weeks behind on the next book that was due to her, but the reason for it had been the rave reviews of his latest book and the number of signing engagements that Aura had been able to set up.

The computer screen was beginning to blur on him. The words were not making a whole lot of sense at this point, but he was determined to get this last chapter done in the next hour. He'd been writing today for well over six hours and he needed a break. He hadn't eaten all day; his stomach was growling but he pushed on. The phone ringing interrupted his flow and forced him to stop.

"Hello?" he'd glanced at the number but didn't recognize it.

"Hi, Baby," Elise answered. "I've missed you and thought I'd call and see how you're doing."

"I don't have time for any bullshit today, Elise," his attempted to remain calm with his ex-wife was failing. "I have a deadline to meet and I'm behind. What do you want?"

"I don't want anything, Graylin," she was miffed by his attitude. "I just wanted to know if I could come over and see you?"

"No," he was blunt with his answer.

"Why not? I could cook dinner for you while you work, and maybe even give you a massage..."

"Again, no, Elise," he pushed back from his computer and wiped his eyes. "I don't have time for this at all. I don't need you calling here, and I don't want you coming by. I want you to just get on with your life and to leave mine the hell alone."

"Why are you doing this, Graylin?" he could hear the tears in her voice and a small part of him wanted to know if it was sincere or just another of those moments when she was merely pushing his buttons. "I need to see you. I need for you to want me to come see you. Why are you pushing me away?"

"Why?" he stood up and walked away from his desk and began pacing his floor. "Why? I cannot believe this shit. Are you fucking serious right now? Elise, I'm going to say this one last time and after this don't fucking call me anymore… We are not together and we're never going to get back together. I don't want to see you; I don't want to fuck you… I don't want to FUCK with you. I want you to leave me alone. PERIOD.

"Do you understand me? Do you get it now? Just… just stop… please." His voice softened, and he was truly pleading with her just hoping against hope that she would finally get it. "I need to go, I have some more writing to do."

"Graylin, please." He hung up before she could say anymore.

"I need a vacation," he walked over to the calendar hanging on the wall behind his desk. The date for him to meet Trinity in Atlanta was circled and it was only three days away, and that was the only thing he was truly concentrating on. He glanced at his watch and turned back to his computer sitting down in his chair; if his timing was right she should be sending him an IM at any time.

He stared at the words on the screen reading through what he'd written, and it wasn't as bad as he'd expected. As he read, he was also thinking what else he needed to pack because he truly had no intensions of doing anything more than enjoying his time away from everything he was so used to… especially shit dealing with Elise.

"Just a few more days," he whispered towards the screen as he looked upon a picture of Trinity he'd pulled up without realizing it. His attention was on her eyes because they always seemed to give off this golden glow. At long last, his computer chimed with an incoming message.

I'm so sorry that I'm late, Daddy. That was quickly followed by smiley face emoticon. *Trying to get the last of all of my local things caught up before I have to get on the plane in a couple of days. Are you still coming?*

I wouldn't miss this time away for anything. his response was quick. Their conversation wasn't long because it was late, and she still had things to take care of. After she'd signed off he settled back into his chair and continued his own work that he figured would take him a few more hours to complete. He had a smile on his face; his conversation with Elise was forgotten, and he was once again looking forward to just getting away for a few days.

Daddy, where are you?
The text message had come at just the right time. Traffic was flowing pretty well along I-75 and he was making good time. He read the message on his phone and trying to keep an eye on the road he quickly punched out a message to her letting her know that he would see her in about an hour. Her return message let him know that she was overly excited and that she couldn't wait for him to get there.

Graylin couldn't stop his thoughts from running around all over the place playing out a million different scenarios surrounding this first meeting. He was uncharacteristically nervous, like a teen meeting his prom date's father and expecting the worst kind of response. He was unsure what she would expect of him, or what she would think the moment she saw him up close and personal. He was wondering if she would be as beautiful as her pictures, and for the first time he was wondering if he'd been "catfished".

"Damn." Graylin turned up the music trying to drown out his thoughts.

The city was coming up ahead and it was beautifully bright against the night sky surrounding it. The skyscrapers always seemed larger than those back home, and a little more congested. He turned on the GPS that was attached to his windshield and it began barking out the directions to the address he'd already programmed in for the W hotel.

The moment his phone rang he immediately thought it was Elise but was quite thankful that it was Mishelle most likely just checking up on him and his writing.

"Hey, Ms. Lady," he said answering his phone.
"Hey, Love, what are you up to?"
"Took the night off to hang out with a few friends of mine and they decided that they didn't want to sit around the house talking so we're out and about."
"That's good," she sounded sincere, "you needed some time away from that damn house and your computer. How's things with that woman?"
"She's pushing my buttons, Shelle," he shook his head and quickly turned down the volume to the GPS. "If this shit keeps up I'm going to need to get a restraining order put on her ass just to keep her away from

my house. The other day I was at the grocery store and when I came out she was parked beside my car waiting for me. I swear I wanted to scream and yell, but I just got in the car and drove off. Get this… she followed me all the way home."

"I keep telling you, that girl is bat-shit crazy. You need to something before she finds a way to hurt you and then I'm going to have to hurt her ass."

"I hear you," he was laughing because he knew Mishelle was serious as all get up. "But, I'm not letting her stupid ass keep me from enjoying my life. When I left I left for good and I'm not going back."

"Good," Mishelle was laughing. "You go and enjoy yourself and I'll call Aura and tell her to leave you alone for the weekend. You get back to work on Monday and we'll talk within the week to schedule everything out. I have a few new things to talk to you about, but I don't want to say shit until I have all of the pieces ironed out."

"Sounds good to me. You have a good weekend because I plan to my damn self."

Their call ended just as the GPS gave him the last turn to the before he was pulling up to the valet area of the W Atlanta-Midtown Hotel. It was truly a beautiful building and he wasted no time in telling the young man to be careful with his automobile. He made his way through the lobby and towards the elevators. After pushing the button, waiting for the car was the longest wait he'd ever made, but the moment the doors opened, and the trip up began… Graylin could feel butterflies struggling to get out of his stomach.

With a loud, obnoxious ding, the doors opened again, and he was on the top floor of the massive building. He'd seen a lot of beauty, but this building was a work of art unlike any he'd ever seen. He stood before the suite door unsure if he was ready for the woman or the room, but he knocked and waited.

"You made it," she was breathtaking as she opened the door in nothing but that Cowboy jersey she'd described to him a dozen or more times. "I was so worried that you'd changed your mind."

Her eyes sparkled turning his knees to jelly as he stepped closer to her. The perfume she wore swept over him and his entire body reacted without a thought as he pulled her into his arms and kissed her as hard as he could. They were both breathing through their noses as lips were mashed and tongues dueled in open mouths. Her fingers were at the back of his neck scratching and holding him in place. His hands were upon her back one sliding up to her neck the other down to her ass lifting her up into his body. He pulled back and stared deeply into her eyes once more.

"Hi," she licked her lips hoping to smooth the lipstick that yet remained.

"Hi," he leaned in and licked her lips as well tasting of her what he could. "You look good enough to eat."

"I hope that you do eat me, Daddy," she bit at the side of her body lip. "All weekend and then some."

He lowered her to the floor and she took his hand leading him into the immaculate suite. He wanted to take it in, but the way her ass moved was all that he could see. She moved through the space until the bedroom opened up before them. There was a huge window with the curtains opened showing the beauty of Atlanta and the bed was illuminated by a host of candles and the city. She reached the edge of the bed and turned to face him as he kept walking until they were nothing more and a breath of air apart. His large hands reached out and she moaned as he palmed her breast and squeezed.

Her jersey floated away leaving her body naked before his eyes and he was staring like a starved man. She moved into his arms and he was attacking her lips down to her neck and leaning back to give him the room to have his way with her breasts. Her nipples rose to the point of hurting and he was biting one and pinching the other causing her to squeeze her thighs tightly together. She's drenched already; her excitement by this man being here with her was beyond anything she could have conceived.

Graylin spins her around and his mouth is on her neck as his fingers are deftly working the buttons on his shirt and his pants until he was as naked pressed against her warm body.

"So big," she panted feeling his length slipping between the cheeks of her ass and she's grinding back against him feeling him grow more. "Oh my god, please, Daddy, please."

Her body is shivering as he pushes her forward over the bed. Graylin is staring down at her body being offered to him as he strokes his dick as it's pressed against her. Her breathing is ragged already, and he can smell her passion and need floating up from between them. He was hungry for her and as he leveled his dick to enter her he still couldn't believe that they were here in this moment right now.

Her moans would forever fill his head as he gently pushed forward splitting her open and watching as he slowly sunk in. She was so hot and so wet that all he had to do was grab her by the waist filling her until her hand flies back trying to stop his advance.

"Goddamn, I love you," she's looking back at him over her shoulder. "Now give it to me, Daddy... I'm ready now and I want it all."

His strokes were deep and steady and as he pulled out he'd gaze down upon the soaked length of his shaft before sliding back into this delicious woman. Her moans were punctuated with a grunt each time he'd tap the entrance to her cervix and her hand would reach back as a plea for him to pull out a bit. Her eyes were closed, and her head was thrown back as he thrusts became quicker and deeper. Her mouth dropped open and she was panting and babbling as he bottomed out with each slap of his groin against her upturned ass. She was so wet that her juices were not only running down their legs but dripping from his swinging scrotum.

Her moans and screams were like a song to him and as her ass trembled he held on to her waist with one hand and the other rose just inches above before quickly striking down.

"Oh, my fucking..." her screams echoed in the spacious room. Trinity looked back and the wild glare in her eyes prompted him to strike her ass once more just, so she could watch him do it.

Graylin moaned and grunted as her pussy tightened and contracted like a hand around his dick. Starting at the head and moving along the shaft he could feel every inch of her insides massaging and sucking at him trying to draw him in deeper even as she was begging him to pull back. He took a hold of her ass and began drilling in hard and fast as she held on to the bed for dear life.

Trinity felt like the breath was being beaten from her lungs as her lover fucked her harder than she'd ever enjoyed. He was thicker and longer than any man she'd ever been with and the pain was euphoric as he pushed her body to the edge of an orgasm she'd never experienced. Her toes were curled into the plush carpeting and her fingers were balled up into the bedspread as he pounded he unmercifully. All of the teasing, all of the fantasies, all of the talking lead to this moment and she reveled in it as her body finally exploded.

His hand left her ass and grabbed her hair and pulled back. He watched as her back arched down pushing her ass up and back as he stroked forward filling her and spreading her open. His breathing was ragged and hers was strained as she began chanting that she was cumming and begging him to cum with her. The moment her pussy squeezed Graylin gave in and growled as he viscously slammed in as hard and as deep as her body allowed and his own orgasm broke the dam.

■■■■

(present day)

Graylin stomped into his house throwing his jacket and keys and kicking at the first table he came across. This had been the worst day of his life and it had only worsened the moment he'd seen her name on one of those files. It had been months now since he'd last talked to Trinity; he's often wondered about her, but just excused it off as she was trying to work things out with her husband their marriage. But, seeing her name on that file only brought back memories of a news report of a Denver businesswoman being killed.\

He stumbled through the house looking around but seeing absolutely nothing as the files on the table kept filling his vision. His head was pounding, and he could hear his heart pounding in his chest and his breathing whistling in his ears. His legs felt weak and ready to just crumple under his weight and his stomach churned. Screaming out he grabbed the nearest thing that he could get his hands on and tossed it.

The crash of his hall table breaking against the wall broke the reverie and his eyes clear just enough for him to see through the tears that were now falling. The table was quickly followed by a number of things he could easily toss as he screamed and tore up his home at the revelation that flooded his head.

"That can't be you," he spat stomping around the trashed living room. "Please, God, no... Not her... Not Her!"

Chapter 7: A Broken Smile

Elise sat slowly in the chair she'd been led to after seeing him in the hall. Her thoughts were all over the map as she reached up and touched her face where his hands had been. His fingers were so soft and gentle as he held her staring at the bruises all over her face... lovingly. His eyes were soft, softer than she'd remembered, and they were not mean or angry.

"Ms. Mannsen?" the voice kept trying to break in on her thoughts, but Elise was trapped standing there staring up at her husband as he caressed her face like he used to. She couldn't breathe, the air was thick in her lungs and stuck in her throat as she tried to keep from crying.

"He still loves me," she whispered before looking up at the cop in the room with her.

"Are you alright, Ma'am?" the cop asked.

"Yes," Elise smiled and placed her hands flat on the top of the table. "Yes, Officer, I'm great."

"The detectives will be in here in a moment," the officer informed her as he moved towards the door.

"Do you know why I've been called back in here?" she tried batting her eyes, but the pain of blinking stopped her quickly. "Or, do you know why my husband was here?"

Immediately, Elise regretted that second question as she thought about the call she'd made earlier and her implications later once the police had arrived at her home. She silently curses and began thinking of excuses for the questions she was sure were soon to follow. She stared at the young cop and tried to smile as he backed out of the room closing the door leaving her with her thoughts.

Damn... I may have fucked up.

She couldn't get his face out of her head. His big brown eyes were like those of a deer caught in the headlights of an onrushing truck, but he didn't let that stop him from examining her face. She was sure he'd memorized every bruise and that made her smile on the inside as she looked up and stared at the mirrored glass across the room from her. She had to remember to play her role because she was sure they were watching and the last thing she wanted to do was show them anything other than what they'd seen earlier... especially, if Graylin was in there with them.

Details, she thought to herself, *I have to remember details. If you get one thing off, Elise, they're going to know, and you go from being victim to suspect.*

The day had flown by and yet the conversation that she'd had with Graylin stuck firmly in her mind. She'd called him like she'd been doing for weeks now, every morning before seven while he was still in bed and not quite awake. He was always more acceptable to her voice first thing in the morning and that was always pleasing because it would be the best way to start her day. It never failed, she'd call him, and her thoughts would always go back to their mornings together before he walked out on her.

Elise took a deep breath and held it as she heard the first sound of his early morning voice. It was always so much deeper first thing and then it would mellow out during the course of the day, but that first thing in the morning voice always excited her. She often wondered if he knew how much just his voice excited her, but it never really mattered because more than his voice could cause her body to melt from the inside out.

"Yea?" She could always tell that he hadn't looked at the screen to see the number. "Who is this?"

"I just wanted to call and tell you to have a good day, Baby."

"Elise? Elise, is that you?"

"Yes, Graylin," she loved saying his name. "I just wanted you to know that I was thinking about you."

"Why do we do this?" He was groggy, and his voice was so deep that it just seemed to rumble through the phone, and she could feel her body tremble.

Elise was laying in her own bed in nothing but a sheer baby doll nightie and staring up at a mirror that she'd mounted to the ceiling. Her nipples were hard and pressed against the thin material, and the moment her fingernail grazed one she had to hold her breath so that she wouldn't gasp. She pinched her nipple as she listened to him breathing before she spoke again.

"Do… what, Graylin?" It was getting harder to control herself with each call. In her mind he was laying there in his boxer briefs and a tank top t-shirt which was his sleeping attire of choice. She could picture him with his legs sprawled as he was laying on his back, and his dick was like a limp road bump in his shorts. Elise licked her lips as the pain from her nipple and her imagination flickered the flame already burning.

"You know what," Graylin calmly answered. "You call every morning and I don't know why. We need to stop torturing each other like this, Baby, it's not good for either of us."

"You could always let me come home to you," she whispered hopefully into his ear. "You could just let me love you. You need me,

Graylin."

"No, Elise," she could hear him moving around in bed and her thoughts quickly traveled down towards his waist and she caught herself before she moaned. "You have to just let me go, Elise, please… We tried to make things work, when you came back I tried to make it all work, but there is no us anymore."

"Don't say that," she was pleading with him again. She hated when he made her beg like this, but he was more receptive when she begged. "I love you, you know that."

"No, Elise," he was being stern now, and again that made her body tremble. She sucked in another deep breath as her fingers slowly made their way down her body towards the hem of her gown. She scratched at her thighs feeling a release of need as the welts burned and rose. She could hear his voice but didn't hear a thing he was saying as her fingers moved up between her spread legs scratching deeper and harder against her over sensitive skin.

Shit… Concentrate, Elise, they're watching you before they come back in here. Get your fucking head back into the game or we're truly fucked.

"Right," Elise whispered hearing her voice before she realized she'd actually spoke aloud.

"Right, what, Ms. Mannsen?" it was the burly cop from earlier… Detective… Marcum.

"Right on time, Detective Marcum," she tried to smile. "I was just sitting here wondering how it would be before someone came in to talk to me."

"I'm sorry that we kept you waiting," Marcum lied. "We had to get a few last things settled with Mr. Cross before allowing him to leave. With everything that you told us earlier, well, the last thing we'd want is for him to skip town or worse yet; come after you again."

"After me?" she feigned confusion. "What do you mean, come after me again?"

Marcum shuffled through his papers as if he was looking for something and then pulled out a single sheet of paper and laid it on the table. He didn't look up at the woman across from him but moved his lips like he was silently reading the page. His fingers laced together with is index fingers steepled beneath his chin.

"Detective?"

"Oh, I'm sorry," he looked up from the paper as he slid it across the table so that she could see it. "According to this police report you filed, we were under the suspicion that it was your ex-husband..."

"We're not divorced, Detective," she corrected him. "We're just separated while we work some things out."

"My apologies, Ms. Mannsen," Marcum sat back in his chair staring at her. "It is Mannsen, yes?"

"For now," Elise relaxed her facial expressions as the man goaded her. "I never went through the process of having my last name changed, but once we hash out our differences that will be one of the first things I get taken care of."

"I see," Marcum leaned forward over the table and pointed at the police report once more. "As I was saying, Ms. Mannsen, according to this report we were led to believe that it was Mr. Cross who beat you."

"Graylin?" Elise glanced down at the paper like she was reading it. "Why on earth would you people think that? Graylin would never put his hands on my like this. My husband loves me, Detective."

On cue, Elise began crying.

So well played, Marcum thought as he again sat back from the table watching. The tears were real as she dropped her head and her body shook with the theatrics of her promotion. He'd seem some damn good shows, but this woman was well practiced and well versed. There was no way they'd be able to hold her, but her recanting her earlier accusation has definitely put her up at the top of his list of suspects.

"What if I told you that Mr. Cross was out of town at the time of your attack?"

"What would that matter, Detective?" her anger was clear. "I just told you that Graylin would never do anything like this to me."

"Do you know who would?" Marcum felt like he was poking a cornered tiger with a short stick, but he needed to get under skin at this point just to see what she would give away.

"God, no." It was a full one hundred and eighty degrees turn in emotions. Her voice was calm, and her attitude dialed down as she resumed her tear-filled play acting. Marcum wasn't convinced.

"Ms. Mannsen," Marcum forced and air of concern, "we need your help in any way with trying to find whoever did this to you. Our initial suspect had been your husband but now we're pretty much at square one. Can you tell us anything about your attacker?"

Details, Elise, remember you have to give them the same details without adding him into the mix. Detail. Details.

"I wish that I could remember everything, Detective," she took a deep breath and sat there thinking, "I mean it all just seemed to happen so fast. One minute I was alone in my bedroom and the next thing I remember is getting my face beaten in like I was in an MMA match. I cannot remember seeing who it was, but I do remember calling out for my husband."

"Do you think," she stared across the table hoping that she was putting on her best sympathetic look, "that that's where your officers mistakenly thought I was blaming my husband?"

"That is a possible assumption," Marcum offered with a shrug. "I'll definitely have to question the officers who first interviewed you to see what their take on it was. What I could use is your thoughts on what happened."

Easy, Elise... the detective is very good at what he does and he's trying to draw you in. Think... Details... Remember everything that you said before.

"I cannot remember, um, exact details," she tried not to stare into the older man's eyes, "but I'll tell you everything that I can."

Drop your head, pretend that you feel responsible. The voice in her head was being very proactive. *You're like a rape victim and this simpleton needs to feel sorry for you just like the two fools earlier.* The voice, her voice, kept her on track and she listened. Her voice became softer and her head dropped, and she added in tears to make it all look and sound appropriate. *Slow and easy, Elise, give him something to hang on.*

"I don't remember everything exactly," she was staring down at the table, "I mean... it all happened so fast. I do know that whoever hit me had big hands. I remember that I hit my head on the side of my dresser and then the back of my head was slammed into the mirror."

Marcum was writing things down as she continued. He reached into his jacket pocket and pulled out the clean handkerchief that his wife always made certain he had and slid it across the table to young "actress" sitting before him. He was unimpressed, but he kept his facial façade as well as she kept hers and continued listening as if he were falling for every word dripping from her lips.

Marcum had memorized her original statement and was impressed that she was able to tell him almost word for word exactly what she'd said before. As he watched her, it was like she was being coached by someone reading the first statement, but he knew that there were no earbuds in with someone speaking to her. He filed that information away in the back of his head for now while she continued with the crocodile tears and the sob story.

"Thank you, Ms. Mannsen," he said at long last glancing down at her 'new statement' before laying it atop the previous. "I'll have my men return you home and we'll put a car outside to keep watch through the night... just in case whoever did this tries to return."

"Thank you, Detective Marcum," she wiped the tears from her eyes once more, "if you feel that is necessary."

"Just for safety's sake," Marcum stood and walked towards the door. "And, you have my number just in case you remember anything, or you need to contact me."

Elise tried to smile and nodded her head gently. She couldn't read this man, his expressions were harder to comprehend than Graylin, but she was almost sure that he'd accepted her revised story. She sat trying not to stare at the mirrored window, but she could feel eyes on her and it was making her uncommonly nervous.

Easy, Elise, the voice was soothing. *We're almost out of here, and when we get home we can call him. Find out why he was out of town. Find out why he hadn't told you that he was going out of town. Just a bit longer, and we'll walk out of here just as we walked in and they'll be NONE the wiser.*

"Yes," Elise said under her breath. *"I'm coming home to you, Graylin, why do you fight me so?"*

Marcum stepped into the observation room where Abraham was watching and waiting. He held out the two statements and shook his head.

"What is it?" Abraham separated the pages and looked them both over.

"She's good," Marcum stated. "Very good, and if I didn't know any fucking better I'd swear someone was telling her what to say."

"Shit," Abraham quickly noticed what he referring to. "She repeated everything excuse where she'd accused her husband of beating her."

"Exactly." Marcum turned to leave the room. "Release her, but I want her ass under constant surveillance. And we need to let Mr. Cross know what we suspect; we can go by and see him in the morning."

"I'll go let the captain know what's going on."

"Yea..." Marcum walked off towards his desk. What he needed right now was a drink, but he'd stopped drinking just a couple of years ago and was fighting to stay clean. He could almost taste a swallow of whiskey washing over his tongue and the sensation of as so strong that he actually got light headed.

"Damn," he pulled out his phone and dialed a number. As he waited for an answer he took a big swig of water trying to wash that alcohol taste from his memory.

"You rarely call, Erick," the voice on the other side of the phone had finally answered after several rings. "I can only assume that you need to talk, yes?"

"Please… Samuel, it's serious."

"There's a meeting in about 45 minutes at the old church," Samuel sighed heavily. "I'll meet you there."

"Thank you. I appreciate this."

Elise walked up to her door and looked back over her shoulder to see where the police would be parking for the night. She tried to smile and waved to let them know she was going inside and the young cop sitting on the passenger side nodded his head letting her know that they would be there if needed.

She opened the door and stepped in immediately hating where she was. The walls were already closing in on her as she dropped her purse and jacket to the floor in front of the door. The quiet was depressing and angered her beyond words as she quickly walked from room to room as if looking for something… Someone. Her heart was racing with hope, but she was quickly disappointed as she remembered one thing.

Graylin didn't know where she lived.

Slowly, she retraced her path back to the office she'd set up with a large window that looked out into the backyard that she'd had equipped with all manner of things a young child would love. There was a huge treehouse erected between three large oak trees and a complete swing and slide like the ones you'd see on the playgrounds. She pulled back the curtains and stared out and smiled as she pictured their children running around and screaming and playing while they sat in the veranda drinking lemonade and watching.

"Be careful, LJ," she could hear Graylin calling out to their little boy named after him, *"don't play to roughly with the girls."*

"Our children are so beautiful, Graylin," she whispered to herself as she pressed her hand to the cool glass. A real tear slowly fell from her eyes as she tried to pull away from the empty backyard but couldn't.

"I fucking hate you… I hate you… I HATE YOU…"

Chapter 8: Time With His Princess

The phone ringing caused him to tense up as he stared at it laying on the nightstand by his bed. He'd just stepped out of the shower and was trying to get his head straight before leaving to go pick up his daughter for the weekend. With nothing but a towel on, Graylin looked around as if he were expecting someone to jump out of the closet at him and this upset him that he was afraid to move around in his house comfortably. He stepped out the doorway of the bathroom and into his bedroom cautiously walking towards the phone.

"Elise?" he'd glanced at the caller ID before answering. "What do you want?"

"Oh, good morning, Love," he could hear the smile in her voice like he should be happy to hear from her. "I just wanted to make certain you slept well."

"Slept well? Now let me think about that."

Graylin walked into the kitchen with the phone stuck to his ear and checked the coffee pot, and at the moment that was the only thing making him smile. He couldn't stop walking around and checking rooms feeling like this woman was watching him somehow or another.

"Graylin, are you still there?"

"Yes, Elise, but the question is, why are you still on the phone? Why do you insist on calling me?" There was a vague attempt to maintain the calmness in his voice as he walked back into his bedroom and sat down on the side of the bed.

"You don't understand, Graylin, I just wanted to hear your voice." Her answer made his sick to his stomach as thoughts of yesterday flooded his thoughts.

"What the fuck do you mean you miss me?" He couldn't stop the flood of words as he dropped his head into his hand. "You fucking told the police I beat you, Elise, you had them believing that I could do something that horrible. Why? Why the hell would you say some shit like that? You know that I'd never do that to you; hell, you tried what, a few times to get me to hit you and what did I do? I walked away."

"I didn't tell them that, Graylin," she was almost begging him to believe her. "They took what I was saying out of proportions. I was in hysterics because someone had gotten into my home and they'd..."

"Beaten the shit out of you," he finished. "Yea, I seen that."

"I'm so sorry that they, that they embarrassed you like that." Elise was trying hard to make him believe that she had nothing to do with them thinking he'd been responsible for her being battered, but Graylin had his suspicions.

"Look, Elise," he took a deep breath, "I'm sorry about what happened to you and I'm sure that at some time we'll have to deal with the fact that the cops think I'm responsible… but right now, I can't deal with this. I need to get up and get dressed because I have some things I need to go do."

"What things, Graylin?" There was a sudden coldness in her voice that was unmistakable. "You going out of town again? You off to see one of your little bitches again?'

"What in the hell are you talking about?" Graylin was up off the bed pacing around taking note that her entire demeanor had changed.

"I know that you went out of town, the police tried to play if off, but I'm not stupid. Where did you go, Graylin?"

"You make it sound like I'm trying to hide shit from you, Elise," he was irate at his point. "Wait… we're not together, goddammit, so I don't have to explain the shit I do to you. What I do is my own goddamn business. Now I'm getting the fuck off of this goddamn phone because I have some place to be.

"Don't call back, Elise… I mean that shit. Don't fucking call me anymore." He hung up the phone just as she'd taken in a deep breath to say something. He wasn't interested in anything else that she could want to say as he contemplated changing his phone number and the shit-storm that would cause with making certain that all of his business associates got the new number. He shook his head as he began to accept that his ex-wife was becoming a problem that he'd have to address eventually.

"Hold on, Kenni," he said aloud as he began looking for something to wear, "Daddy's coming, Princess."

Graylin pulled up to the house and sat there for a moment just trying to collect himself. He'd spent last night drinking heavily, and he'd missed his alarm going off. He'd just barely managed to get up and get showered while still trying to come to grips with the shit from yesterday. His brain was still spinning with thoughts of being hauled into the police station and questioned about Elise being beaten badly, but he'd been out of town on a small book tour that Aura had put together at the last minute.

He shook his head trying to shake the thought of talking to Elise's ass this morning, but the conversation still left a bitter taste in his mouth.

He glanced around the neighborhood, but the feeling that she was somewhere rattled his nerves. After a moment he laughed and through himself stupid because... *There's no way she could be here,* he said in his head. *I never told her about Sadè and Kennadey.*

"Damn," he groaned a little as he pulled off his sunglasses and allowed the full burst of the sun's like to finally hit them. Looking around again he was taking in everything he'd left behind when he moved from this neighborhood several years ago and he smiled. His first ex-wife was given the house and of course a car because he wanted to make certain that his daughter had a stable home to be in.

"It's almost like saying, 'home, sweet home'," he shut off the car and opened his door.

There was a slight breeze that caught the smells from the old fashion donut shop that was up the block making him hungry and sick at the same time. He grabbed the cup of really, strong black coffee and took another swig before stepping out of the car. He turned and leaned against the top of his car for a moment just making certain that he wouldn't lose neither his balance nor the contents in his stomach. Checking his watch, Graylin couldn't help looking around one last time and shook his head; there were absolutely no children out on such a beautiful and perfect Saturday morning.

It was early yet, but still...

"Damn, what I wouldn't give to be a kid on a day like this," he said sweeping his eyes around at the houses and yards around him. "Crazy children don't know what they're missing being all stuck up in the house."

This was his Saturday to get his daughter Kennadey, and he was always sure to come early because his ex, Sadè, had no problems with changing her plans and taking off even if she knew he was coming over. They'd been having this dance going on five or six years now, and you'd think he would be used to her being petty but her doing things never failed to irritate the hell out of him. Shaking his head, he wondered about the choices he'd made in picking women, and almost laughed.

"Bad," he said quickly. "All fucking bad, you'd think that after two failed marriages you'd realize that."

The argument he had with himself on a normal basis. He and Sadè married young, way too young, and way before he was ready to be married. As his mother would tell him, that's what happens when you're playing house and she winds up pregnant. He had to handle his responsibilities and for a little while it seemed like it was the right choice. They'd been married when she was about seven months or so pregnant and she made such a beautiful bride with her off white dress and her belly poking out; he'd even stood before the preacher holding her belly through most of the ceremony.

He was happy. He was going to be a dad and he was going to be a damn good husband. He was happy, but she wasn't, and she never told him. He'd found them the perfect little starter home and he went into so much debt coming up with the down payment and eventually had to work two jobs just to keep the mortgage up. Sadè stayed home with Kennadey because they couldn't afford sending her to a daycare, but Graylin was determined to give his baby girl the best of everything. They had an old beat up, beat down Toyota Camry that just barely got him to and from work, and he also had an old ten-speed bike that he'd use when she had to take the baby to doctors' appointments.

He was happy.

"Goddammit, Graylin," he hadn't seen her opening up the door, "are you going to stand out there all morning? I have shit I need to go do."

It was a lie, but it was done to make him feel bad; to make him feel like he was the reason she was still at home. There'd been a few times he'd thought about hiring a private investigator to follow her when he had Kennadey just to see where the fuck she'd run off to, but he quickly decided that it would have been a waste of money. She was standing there with that look of disgust on her face that he'd come to love. Her hair was pulled back from her face hanging in a ponytail that almost touched her shoulders and her arms were folded over her boobs as if she were trying to hide them.

Good luck with that, he thought smiling as he pictured her naked. For a slender woman, Sadè was very well-endowed chest wise; he'd never stole a glimpse into her bra for a size, but the fuckers were bigger than his hands could encompass, and they were one of his favorite features about her.

"I'm coming, Allie, I'm coming."

"I've told you about calling me that, Graylin," she was almost snarling. "You lost all rights to nick names when you left."

"Correction, Sadè," he was standing at the foot of the steps looking up at her. "I didn't leave; you walked out on me… twice. After the second time I just decided that I wasn't running after your ass again."

"Whatever… you, selfish bastard."

"How the hell am I selfish?" he feigned being hurt, teasing and watching as she smiled. He was up the three steps before she could say anything else and kissed her on the cheek. "Morning, Grumpy, is my baby up yet?"

"Is she up?" Sadè stood there staring at him like he was crazy. She was wearing the oversized football jersey that she's stolen from him years ago and nothing else as she stood in the door waiting for his ass to walk in. "You do realize what time it is, don't you? It's Saturday and not even seven yet, shit, I shouldn't be up yet. And what's with the kiss on the cheek shit? Boy, get in the house."

Graylin could hear her breathing in his cologne as he squeezed by her. She'd dropped her arms and the softness of her breasts pressed against his arm and he couldn't help the smile. Her nipples were hardening, and he was sure it wasn't just because of the early morning breeze, but because he was there before Kenni had gotten up. He actually loved morning like these.

"What more would you like?" he was grinning as made his way into the kitchen following the smell of fresh coffee. "I do have a cup of half consumed coffee out in the car I could go out and get for you."

"You are such an ass," she was standing behind him as he turned to say something else, but her lips stopped him before he could utter another word. He remembered kisses like this between them and his arms wrapped around her back holding her body to his. They were always so good apart, but together it was like lighting a stick of dynamite and holding it in your hand as it exploded. Her tongue had slipped into his mouth, and his tongue welcomed it. Their lips mashed together. Her hips were gyrating gently, and she was moaning softly into his mouth.

"You're going to start something that you're not going to want to finish," he'd pulled away licking his lips and staring into his ex-wife's pretty, brown eyes.

"You know," she reached out cupping her hand over the growth stretching the front of his pants, "I ain't never afraid to finish anything that I start."

"See, here's the problem," he tried not to give in to her teasing him, "I never said that you were afraid, Sweetheart. I think the word used was... wouldn't."

"And why... wouldn't I?" Her hand was massaging him through his pants as she leaned in to kiss at the exposed part of his chest beneath his shirt. Her tongue was hot, soft and wet as the tip traced a line up his chest and over his chin to press her lips to his once more.

"Why are you teasing me this morning, Sadè?" Graylin felt like silly putty in her hand. She knew just what to do to him to keep his attentions exactly where she wanted them, and this morning it was obvious she wanted his attention on her in ways they hadn't been in a while. He heard the zipper on his pants being pulled down, and before he could stop her...

"Goddamn," she'd pulled her lips away and looked down. "I'd forgotten what you was walking around with. Pisses me off that you're giving this away to someone else."

Graylin hand a hand on the counter with his fingers wrapped around the edge to keep from falling over. Her hands were so fucking soft. She was stroking his length with both hands slowly and making certain that she paid close attention to how her hand would curl around the head. She was staring back into his eyes, but he could hardly see her. He hadn't been her first, but he'd taught her more about pleasing not just a man but herself than any man had ever shown her.

Holding on to him gently, Sadè began walking out of the kitchen with Graylin in tow. She could feel his eyes on her ass bouncing freely beneath the short shirt and she smiled taking him into the living room. Turning to him, she pushed him down onto the sofa and quickly removed her shirt giving him an eyeful of her naked body beneath. He smiled as she slapped his hands away when he reached out for her.

"Easy there, Cowboy," she leaned down and began unbuckling his belt and helping him out of his clothes. "I've missed all of this, and I've been thinking of just how I could get you naked one more time."

"You could have just asked."

"Unlike that crazy bitch you're with," she slowly straddled his lap, "I know about her."

Graylin slid his hands around her back and grabbed her butt giving it a squeeze. She'd always complained about not having a big ass, but he'd always loved everything about her especially her breasts. Leaning in, he sucked on her nipple and she moaned out. Her body was always so receptive to him. He licked at her with the tip of his tongue before nipping with his teeth; her body pressed down upon his length soaking him. She was always so hot.

"Make me scream, Graylin," she whispered over him holding his head into her breast. "I want you so goddamn bad."

Rolling them over on the sofa, Graylin kneeled up between her spread legs. It had been a long time since he'd been here, and she was as beautiful as he remembered. They knew how to please one another, that had always come naturally for the, but they didn't know how to make each other happy together. Sliding slowly into her, he watched her eyes roll back and for a fleeting moment he found himself wondering...

Could we make it work this time?

Sadè was all smiles as she stood and tried smoothing back her hair. Slipping back on her shirt to cover up her sweaty body, she felt like she was on cloud 9. He was still the best she'd had, and he knew how to make her body sing. It was so easy to hate him, even treat him like shit at times... but he really wasn't a bad guy. She still loved him, but he'd never know that.

"Ok," she watched as he too got dressed, "I'll go get your daughter and you can go in the kitchen and fix us some breakfast... deal?"

"Deal."

■■■■

Elise sat on the edge of her bed staring at the cell phone still in her hand wondering what the hell had just happened. It had been a long time since the last time he was so... so, mean to her. The back of her hand was wiping away the tears falling from her eyes as she thumbed the screen of the phone. She wanted to call him back to explain that the police had misunderstood her. She wanted to apologize. She wanted to make him understand.

"Understand," she whispered as she sniffled. "Understand, what?"

Elise stood from the bed and walked around to the window that faced the front of her house. The police car was still sitting there, and the two cops were not the same from last night when they'd dropped her off; there'd been a shift changed, and she hadn't been paying attention. She stared back down at the phone and his number was back on the screen. Had she done that and not noticed? She wanted to hear his voice and to know that he wasn't mad at her. She needed him to...

The temptation was to throw her phone, wipe her eyes and say to hell with him. The GPS notification that she'd set up secretly on his phone went off letting her know that he was no longer at home, and she frowned; why hadn't this gone off when he'd gone out of town? If it had she wouldn't have said as much to the police if she'd known that he wasn't home. She cursed under her breath.

"Understand," her voice was sharper, it was harder and angry. "Fuck him understanding."

Elise stood at the window watching the unmarked cop car on the street below as she dialed a new number. As she waited, the tears ceased to flow, and her smile returned. One the third ring a female's voice answered.

"I need you," Elise was blunt. "Come to the house and use the trail through the back. I'll leave the back-garage door open for you."

"I'll be there in ten minutes."

Ten minutes was just enough time for her to get dressed and be ready. Amelia has never failed her, and it's always helped that they favored so closely that she could leave her best friend here at the house and the police would swear it was her. She needed to know where he was going, and who he was going to see so early in the day. Today would be a sloppy day that way he wouldn't recognize her, so it was sweats, a ball cap and some big shades. She pulled he hair back into a ponytail and slipped on a pair of sneakers and waited for the door to close letting her know that Amelia was there.

"There are cops outside," she told the woman who just happened to be a couple of inches shorter than herself, but with her hair down and from a distance…who could tell. "Just walk by the windows every so often until I get back to let them think I'm still here."

"Where are you going, Elise?" Amelia sounded concerned. "You're not going to see him, again are you?"

"No," Elise lied. "I just need to get the hell out of here for a while, and I don't need a fucking police escort. Can you do this for me, please?"

"You know I will," Amelia tried to smile at her friend as she handed her the keys to her car. "Just please, please be careful."

"I'm always careful."

Elise sprinted from the house and down the small path that ran down the back side of her home and her backyard neighbor's home. Amelia had parked her car just down the road, the red Toyota Camry wasn't something that she would own so it would hide her from his eyes just in case they happened to get too close. He would never suspect her drive anything other than her Excursion because he knows how much she loves that huge truck.

After sliding into the driver's seat, she checked the GPS again and was quickly on the road following the direct path to where ever it was he'd finally come to a stop. According to the quick calculations the service provided, Graylin had driven about twenty minutes south of his house and that would put him in the neighborhood that he'd shown where he'd grown up.

"Why are you there?"

Traffic was ridiculous and yet didn't slow her as she whipped the car through tight spots weaving her way towards her husband and his unusual trip to the south side of town. After she'd moved to be with him and before he'd left her to be alone, Elise could count the number of times on one hand that Graylin had ever talked about going to that side of town. He'd moved his mother closer to his current neighborhood just, so he wouldn't have to go there, and his brother and sister both lived in neighboring suburbs away from the slum they'd all known as children. Her thoughts of that side of town turned her stomach as she could only imagine him going down there to be with some slut he'd known years and years ago.

The GPS pointed the direction and with each turn she drew closer to where he'd stopped and was quite surprised that the area didn't look as bad as she'd recalled. The houses were neither small nor ransacked shacks that needed to be torn down and rebuilt; instead the homes were quite large all sporting well-manicured yards and clean streets. This was not the place she'd remembered Graylin bringing her to, and as she pulled up on the street where she spotted his car... she was absolutely positive that he'd never brought her to this side of town.

"What are you doing here?" she slowed the car down and parked so that she could watch his car in her rear-view mirror. "Who the hell are you visiting?"

She sat waiting for him and didn't have too long to wait as the door of the beautiful, wood home opened, and he stepped out. She watched in shock as her husband turned and kissed the gorgeous, black woman on the lips before taking the small hand of the beautiful little girl at his side. Her eyes stretched as the unlikely couple walked towards his car and the woman stood in the doorway waving her hand as the little girl waved back. She noticed the backpack slung over his shoulder just before he pulled it off and tossed it into the backseat before helping her into the car and strapping her down; she estimated her to be about nine, and for the first time she wondered...

"A child?" You bastard!" she was sitting in the car screeching. "You have a goddamn child. You have a goddamn child."

Chapter 9: Another Lesson to Teach

Her anger was beyond appeasing, and her home for the last two or three days could attest to that fact. After returning home secretly from spying on her husband, Elise stormed through her home like a hurricane destroying anything in her path. She'd warned her friend to leave and once she was alone in the house her rage took over. Her kitchen was first and all of the plates and glasses in the cabinets went flying. The sound of the breaking dishes was like music and served as the fuel she desired.

The destruction carried over into other parts of the house as chairs, tables and even mirrors fell before her. She stomped around screaming at the top of her lungs as something fragile slammed against the wall falling in a heap at her feet. The commotion had gotten loud enough to catch the attention of the two policemen sitting outside her home. It had taken them a moment of pounding on the door and her not answering for one of the men to finally kick the door in and the two men rushed through the house looking for her.

"Ms. Mannsen," the two men echoed the other as they came through with their weapons drawn.

"Are you alright, Ma'am," the younger looking of the two called out as he glanced at his partner and nodded for him to go off in the opposite direction he was walking. "Ms. Mannsen, it's Officer Raymonds, Ma'am... are you ok?"

"Yes," she was winded as she stepped out into the living room area where the cop was. "Sorry, I got a bit of bad news and I just kinda, um, took it out on the furniture."

"The house is clear, Partner," the other cop had entered the room from the same direction she'd come out of. "The house's a little worse for wear, but we're good."

Elise had smiled hoping that the two cops would just leave her home, and as she walked them out she took note of the door. Closing it as best she could she turned the deadbolt lock hoping that it would hold until she could contact someone to fix it all for her. Walking back through her home she kicked around the pieces of a broken vase cursing the mess she'd made, and for the next couple of days she'd done nothing to clean it up.

"I'll call the maid service and have them clean this shit up," she'd said to herself a few times, but hadn't pulled out her phone to call anyone.

Sitting in the darkened living room and staring at the wall, Elise tried not to think about Graylin, but failed. Her every thought was always about him in one way or another; and this time it was him, that woman, and that little girl. Her heart was hurting because she'd always pictured them having children together, and that never went away even thought he'd walked away. It was nothing for her to hear two or three children running through the house screaming and playing as she and Graylin watched them with smiles on their faces.

Tears were falling from her eyes and she didn't attempt to wipe them away.

"Why, Graylin?" her words hung in the air around her. "I love you, you son-of-a-bitch. I fucking love you."

Standing, she stomped around the living room until she was before a wall that she'd punched a hole into. A finger slowly traced around the ragged edges as she sniffled. As her finger was coming full circle, she smiled. Facing the wall, Elise drove her forehead into the plaster and exhaling a deep breath as she rested her head against the broken wall.

Her phone's text message notification sounded, and she grabbed the phone glancing at the screen angrily. For a moment she'd hoped it was Graylin texting to apologize, but it wasn't him. She didn't recognize the number, but the part of the message that she could read intrigued her to open it to see it all.

You know that he's playing you. I can help you get back at him if you'd like to and all it would take is for you to go to the airport and collect the ticket already purchased in your name. I think it's time to teach him another lesson. What do you think, Elise?

"Yea, looks like someone is ready," she was laughing as she pounded her forehead into the plaster again and again until blood mixed with the tears. "Yes, yes… it's time for another lesson. You have to learn, Graylin, you have to learn."

■■■

"Excuse me, Mrs. Wheeling," Trinity looked up as Darwin poked his head in to get her attention.

"Yes," she laid her pen down and sat there rubbing her temples. "Why are you still here, Darwin?"

"I was getting ready to leave, but there was someone knocking at the door saying she needed to see you," he quickly explained. "She said that it was important, Ma'am."

"Who is it? Do I know her?"

"I do not think so," Darwin glanced down at the paper that he was holding. "Her name's Elise Mannsen."

Trinity rolled the name around in her head for a moment before she realized where she'd heard it. Sitting back in her chair, she smiled. How did this woman find out about her, let alone find her, and the fact that she'd traveled there to actually see her? Should she be astounded or fucking terrified?

"Now this should be quite interesting," she licked her lips as she told Darwin to show her guest in.

Trinity had asked an abundant number of questions about his ex-wife, and Graylin gave them freely. They'd spent hours upon hours on the phone talking about their lives and their spouses so there was absolutely nothing that this woman could say to her that could or would surprise her. The one thing that she was concerned about was that Graylin had warned her several times that Elise was dangerous and not to be taken lightly.

"Excuse me again, Mrs. Wheeling," Darwin had opened the door stepping in before the woman walking up behind him. "This is Ms. Elise Mannsen; Ms. Mannsen, this is Mrs. Wheeling."

Trinity watched as the haughty woman stepped around her personal assistant and into her office. Trinity stood, and the two women appraised one another much like a jeweler evaluating a diamond. Trinity noted how beautiful Elise's blue eyes were with her long dark hair flowing down past her shoulders and the way her dress looked painted onto her body. Elise stared Trinity with her short hair feathered in a controlled, wild way and her eyes sparkled like gold and her smile was completely unnerving.

Trinity pointed to the chair before her desk and as Elise made her way across the room she released Darwin, reluctantly, for the night.

"Welcome."

"So," Elise couldn't take her eyes off of the woman, "you're her?"

"I'm... who?"

"I've come quite a ways to see you, Mrs. Wheeling, please... do not insult my intelligence. I know exactly who you are, and I'm pretty sure you have an inkling as to whom I may be."

"Not to insult you in any way," Trinity smiled, this would be like any other business meeting she's ever been involved in, "I know exactly who you are, and I must say, he didn't describe you properly."

"How long have you been seeing my husband, Mrs. Wheeling?" Elise bluntly asked. Her eyes never wavered from those of the other woman as she was determined to get answers.

"Two things, Ms. Mannsen, seeing is quite what I'd call what Graylin are and have been doing, and second; your... husband?" Trinity mocked her. "Don't you mean your ex-husband?"

"We are still married, so no," Elise took a deep trying to remain calm.

"Are you sure that's what you want to know?" Trinity was leaning on her desk her smile broadened. "Graylin and I have had some wonderful moments. You almost ruined a great man."

"Answer my question, Bitch."

"What question, Ms. Mannsen?" Trinity was close to laughing as her lover's ex sat squirming in her seat. "You never took his name, how stupid are you. When he told me that I thought he was just saying that for my sympathy, and yet here you are making demands when you don't have a leg to stand on."

"You are pissing me off."

"And I, Ms. Mannsen, don't give a damn."

Trinity sat back in the large, over stuffed leather chair. Beneath the desk she'd crossed her legs, and her arms were folded across her chest and she hoped she appeared calm and reserved. Her heart was pound like a drum in her chest so loud she was sure that the other woman heard it, but she maintained her smug look. Her blood was rushing through and ringing in her ears, and she could feel the cool air on her forehead. She waited for the explosion.

"I'll ask this last time" Elise sat forward on the edge of the chair, "how long have you been fucking my goddamn husband?"

"Let me put it this way, Ms. Mannsen," Trinity mirrored Elise sitting on the edge of her seat, her lips pulled away from her teeth making her smile ominous, and her eyes flashed maliciously. "My pussy is in love with the way that cock of his can stretches me open in ways no man ever has."

Elise moved, and the swing happened faster than Trinity could react. Elise's hand connected with the side of her face, and Trinity couldn't resist letting the laugh she'd been holding on to erupt in the woman's face.

"Mm, bravo, Baby, bravo." Trinity rubbed her face. "I'd been wondering about and I must say.... you hit like a bitch."

With a huff, Elise stood. The two women squared off with the desk between them keeping them each from reaching out for handful of hair. Trinity's smile had lessened, and her eyes narrowed as she now knew that her lover's ex-wife didn't mind taking a swing at her, but now she wondered just how far Elise would go.

"I'll only tell you this once, Mrs. Wheeling," Elise's voice had lowered as she stepped back around the chair she'd been sitting in, "stay away from Graylin. I will not tell you again."

"I'm afraid, Ms. Mannsen, that you have no say in who Graylin Cross fucks," she licked her lips watching as her new adversary shook at her words. "As a matter of fact, I think it's you who should stay away from him. He left you for a reason, and I honestly think it's because your ass is crazy."

"You have no idea just how crazy," Elise's lips turned up into a sadistic looking smile. "But, if you'd like to find out… go near my husband again."

"I think that it's time for you to leave," tired of the back and forth of the dead-end conversation, Trinity dismissed the woman. "Don't come back or I will have you arrested for harassment."

"Like I said, stay away from him."

Not waiting for any kind of a response, Elise stormed from the office with Trinity staring after her. Her blood was boiling at the thought of her husband sleeping with such a brash woman and thinking that it wouldn't have an effect on her. The cool night air felt good against her skin as she walked to the rental car waiting for her curbside. Looking back at the building housing the Wheeling business office, Elise smiled nodding her head as if agreeing to something unspoken.

"Hello, Babe," Trinity was rocking the large office chair, "guess who just visited me."

"Visited you… where?" Graylin was confused.

"Here at my main office," Trinity answered with a nervous laugh. "She was just here, and we had a very lively conversation. I take it that you didn't know she'd left town?"

"I don't keep up with her ass," he was beyond pissed off. "But, that's not the problem; how the fuck did she know about you, that is my goddamn problem. It's not like we sit around discussing who I'm fucking."

"Well just from the fact that she was here I'd definitely say that she's keeping some pretty close tabs on you, Graylin. You may want to get someone to go through your computer and your cell phone to see if she's got some spyware on either or both of them."

"How bad was it?" he asked.

"Not too bad," Trinity was actually grinning, "although, she did slap me, but beyond that it was pretty much just some empty threats. You need to be careful, Graylin, she calls you her husband; meaning, she's not accepting your separation. A woman like that can become very dangerous."

"What do you mean… very dangerous?"

"Ever seen that movie with Glenn Close, Fatal Attraction?"

"Yea," Graylin answered before realizing what Trinity was getting at. "Damn. You need to be careful yourself. Elise showing up there was her way of letting you know that you're on her radar. She doesn't do thing half way, Trin, get you some more people to keep an eye on you."

"I don't scare easy, Lover, and I'm sure she saw that first hand."

"Just be careful," Graylin stressed. "Elise is fucked up in the head and I don't want you caught up in the middle of all of our shit."

Elise pressed the button on her Bluetooth cutting off anymore of the conversation between her husband and that snotty bitch she'd just left. She wiped her eyes of the tears after hearing Graylin concern for another woman over her. For him to tell anyone she was crazy should have angered her, but she was hurt beyond anything.

"Hello?" she'd dialed her friend Amelia without realizing that she had.

"El, you ok?"

"He knows that I'm here, Milli."

"Knows that you're where, Elise?" Amelia was quickly concerned about what her friend may have done. "Where are you?"

"I'm here, in Denver," Elise responded. "I had to see her. I had to let her know that I know about them. I had to tell her to leave my goddamn husband alone."

"Elise, you need to come home," Amelia said trying to get her friend's attention. "You need to come home right now before something happens."

"It's too late, Milli," Elise was crying. "It's way too late."

"Oh my God, Elise… what have you done?"

Nothing… she thought to herself. Nothing yet, but the bitch is going to die.

"It is so good to see that you can follow instructions so well, Elise," she watched as Elise sat in her car. She wondered who she was talking to, and almost dared to guess that it was Graylin. "No, you wouldn't call him, you're too worried that the bitch upstairs would call him. Maybe it's the little nursemaid that you love to use, Amelia… yea, I bet that's who it is. Now you're worried that he knows."

You need to get back home, Elise. The text message showed up in the middle of her conversation. *You don't need to be here any longer.*

Who is this? Elise replied to the text message. *Why are you telling all of this? What are you going to do?*

She sat there staring at her phone wondering if she should tell Elise what was about to happen to Mrs. Grey, but that would take away from the fun of watching her as everything slowly began to unfold. She was the perfect pawn in this little game that she was playing with him. He needed to learn his place in the whole scheme of things, and she was the one to teach him. She pulled up the keyboard on her phone and her dark red lips slipped back into a sly grin.

Trust me when I say that you're going to love what's going to happen. Just keep an eye on your mailbox... you're going to get something very special in a couple of days. It's sure to put a smile back on your face.

I don't know if I like this. I hate not knowing what's going on... Elise quickly typed out. *At least tell me who you are so that I can thank you for all of the information that you've sent me so far...*

I'll tell you soon enough, but for now you need to leave Denver. You go home, and I'll contact you in a few days I give you my word.

"You do follow instructions well," she said watching as the car she'd been watching pulled off. Aura ran her fingers through her spiked hair as Elise slowly drove by her none the wiser. This game was getting to be really fun with this woman. It amazed her at how easily she could be pushed around. "Yes, this is about to get really good."

■■■■

The photo album lying on her lap was old and worn. The front was tattered, and the upper corner was ripped away from the spine. Her mom had bought the book the week before she was born and had kept pictures of her growing up in the book through her college years; from there Elise had taken and added pictures of her own including her most important pictures of her wedding to Graylin. Pictures of her being born had been taken by her father, who had managed to keep from passing out no matter how bloody things had gotten, thus impressing the doctor and the nurses. There were pictures of her first few days as she and her mother had to stay cooped up in the hospital because she'd come a few weeks too early.

Of course, her mother was one of those mothers who took pictures of everything so there was the customary naked baby in the tub shots, and the first day of daycare with her crying her head off and of course that first day of elementary school. Elise had looked through that book so many times that not only were the book covers worn, but the plastic sleeves inside were coming apart just as bad. It was almost a daily ritual to pull the book out and look through the pictures just to keep her head on straight. It never failed; the moment she began her trek down memory lane she'd always leave tears in the book on those pictures that meant the most to her.

Flipping through the book, she was all smiles at the pictures of her childhood. There was a picture of her on a swing being pushed by her dad, which in itself was rare because he hated taking pictures. She stared at him leaning over her on the swing with his super big smile getting ready to push her, and she couldn't stop the flow of tears; he'd died years ago, but this one picture never failed to remind her that he loved her.

"Why did you have to leave me, Daddy?"

I haven't left you, Little Girl, she could almost hear him whispering in her ear. *You know I'd never truly leave you, you're Daddy's little angel.*

"Yes, I am..." she flipped the pages until she got to her wedding and stopped to stare at Graylin.

They were so happy that day, and he looked absolutely gorgeous. He'd opted for the all-white tuxedo with a forest green vest decorated with the silver, paisley filigree. He'd gone out and found his favorite shoes, a pair of black and white Stacy Adams, and he'd gone with an all-white fedora to finish out his look. He looked so dashing that day, like he'd stepped out a magazine from the 1930's just to marry her. She'd never loved another man more than she loved Graylin.

The next couple of pages were just a preview of the perfect life that they had together before he decided to leave her. He left her, just as he reminded her... he left her, and he needed to be reprimanded. He needed to be reminded why they were a great couple. He needed to be reminded that she loved him more than she loved life itself.

"He left me," she repeated to herself again and again as she continued flipping pages until she came to the one she wanted to see. The picture was of that haughty woman she'd confronted, and there was a huge red marker X over her face.

"I'd tried, Graylin," she was gently stroking the face of the picture like the woman was real. "I... I warned her. I told her to leave you alone. I told her that you were still mine and that we were still married. Your little whore wouldn't listen. The bitch laughed at me, Graylin, and all I wanted to do was talk. She had to learn, Baby, I needed her to understand that...

"You're mine, and if I cannot have you..."

The newspaper article's headline that was in the next picture sleeve read, *Local Business Woman and Philanthropist Murdered.*

Elise smiled as she continued to stroke the pictured face of Trinity Grey. The picture had been sent by her new unknown friend letting her finally see who it was that had her husband's attention, but she wasn't the only one. This picture along with pictures of the woman she recently found out was his first wife and pictures of another woman that she hadn't seen in years had also arrived undoubtedly by her same unknown benefactor.

She flipped the pages until she came across the black woman he'd once been married to and their daughter; both were beautiful, and the little girl was like seeing a mirrored image of him. She wiped away a tear and continue through her album until she was staring at the beautiful face of the lovely little brunette looking up at her with those soft, doe brown eyes and her smile spread across her face. She traced the younger woman's face with the tip of her fingernail making a mental note of every line.

"It's been a long time, but we'll be seeing each other very soon, LynMarie," she whispered to the picture. "I'll give you the same chance I gave the first one. I'll have to remind you that he's mine now and always.

"Like I said, dear husband of mine," she continued stroking the girl's photographed face, "you need to be taught another lesson…"

Chapter 10: Do You Know your Wife

"Thank you for coming in, Mr. Cross," Capt. Rowlings had walked from behind her desk to shake his hand. "I think you remember detectives Marcum and Abraham, they're leading the investigation concerning Ms. Mannsen's attack."

Graylin didn't speak but nodded his head acknowledging everyone in the room. He walked towards the chair offered to him by the captain taking note that he wasn't being interrogated in the small room he was in before. The captain's office was nicely designed around the large, stained oak desk sitting back near the wall across from the door. His eyes took in everything quickly before he eased down into the chair.

"So," Graylin glanced from the captain to her two officers noticing that Marcum was staring at him as if waiting for something to happen, and Abraham was once again sizing him up. "So, what's this all about? I mean, you already know that I was out of town when this happened to Elise, and I have people who can corroborate that I was with them at the time…"

"Yes," Rowlings stopped him midsentence. "We're good on all of that, Mr. Cross, everything was confirmed when you were last here."

"Then what?" Graylin was confused and frustrated. The only good thing about being here this time was that he hadn't been dragged in like a criminal. He sat back in the chair, crossed his legs and waited for an answer.

"We've come up with some things that we don't quite have answers for," Rowlings spoke up, "and we were hoping that you could help us fill in the blanks."

"Such as?"

"Such as," Marcum came around and sat on the edge of the desk, "how well do you know your wife, Mr. Cross."

"First… she's my ex-wife," Graylin cleared that up quickly. "Second, to be honest, I thought I knew her quite well but something's not right."

"What do you mean, Mr. Cross?" Marcum asked.

"When I saw her here the other day, her face was all beaten and yet," Graylin hesitated, "there was something in her eyes that made me feel that maybe she…"

"Did that to herself?" Abraham finished for him.

"Yes," Graylin dropped his head shaking it. "She looked so empty, but she was completely thrown off with me being here. What's going on here?"

"Our investigation is coming up with very little on your wi--... on your ex-wife's past." Rowlings said shuffling through a folder before her. "There's no birth certificate, no active social security number; we cannot find a high school, or college, or trade school that knows of her. So again, what do you know about your ex?"

"Just what she told me," Graylin was looking between the three cops extremely confused. "She told me that she lost both of her parents when she was really young and was raised by her grandmother in Amarillo. Her grandmother was the only relative she ever had, and she died when Elise was in her early 20's so I never met any family. As far as I know, she hasn't even been to Amarillo since we got together."

"So, you don't know of another husband?"

"Another... wait, what?" Graylin was sitting on the edge of his seat.

"Well, she didn't tell us of one, but," Rowlings pulled out a piece of paper and slid it across the table, "we found this."

Graylin took the paper and stared at the face of the man on there. The man's name was Terrence Kaine, and the more he studied the man's features the more familiar they became.

"He kind of looks like you, doesn't he, Mr. Cross?" Rowlings stated the obvious. "And there's something more."

"What more could there possibly be? I mean, damn. I never even thought to ask her if she'd been married before, but that's some shit that most people tend to tell you. Why would she keep this from me?"

"So, you don't know about the child?" Marcum asked.

Graylin shook his head.

"She named the boy, Graylin after you." Marcum dropped that bomb in his lap. "She's undoubtedly had a thing for you for a very long time."

Graylin felt like his eyes were bugging out as he continued staring at his "twin". The man had his complexion, his eyes were shaped identical, his thick lips and even his father's aquiline nose. The man's head was shaped like his, and he had the mustache and trimmed goatee.

"Where is this... this... guy?" Nothing was making sense and his words stumbled out of his mouth.

"That's the thing, Mr. Cross," Marcum stood and paced the floor, "Terrence Kaine is dead. According to the coroner's first report he'd died of a heart attack, but the man was in excellent shape."

"You said the first report," Graylin looked up. "What does that mean? Was there another examination done?"

"The family had been screaming foul play since the beginning, and they finally got the state's D.A. to reopen the case and exhumed the body for a new autopsy."

"What's with the dramatic pause?" His frustration was through the ceiling and he just wanted them to spill it all out on the table, so he could digest everything. "What did they find and how does this involve Elise?"

"The new autopsy determined that Kaine died of an overdose of pure nicotine and that's what made it appear as if he'd had a heart attack. The family had been openly stating that it was Elise, but by this time she'd left the state and was off the grind for almost five years."

Graylin felt like his head was about to explode. As a writer, this was the kind of stuff he wrote about; only the cops would have been questioning him as a potential suspect. Somehow, she'd fucked up. She was actually crazier than he'd thought, and he was caught up right in the middle of all this shit.

"So, did she do it?" He finally asked.

"We honestly do not know... yet," Rowlings answered. "We're now doing a more thorough investigation because we're coming up with more questions than answers, and now some new things are coming up and they're surrounding some women we've found are connected to you."

Graylin looked up and stared at each of the three people watching him intently. He could tell that they were waiting to see his reaction, but what they didn't know is that he'd seen the file that had Trinity's name on it. He'd spent the entire night after that looking up things about her case. His main question now is they're thinking that Elise is somehow either a murderer or involved.

"She'd gone to see Trinity Wheeling in Denver," he blurted out. "Did you know that?"

"You just verified a suspicion," Marcum answered. "We'd been in touch with the homicide detectives, and their first thought was that Mrs. Wheeling had had a heart attack on her way home from her office that night. The coroner was ready to sign off on the autopsy when a puncture wound behind her ear was found."

"Pure nicotine?" Graylin voice was trembling.

"Yes," Marcum stated. "How did you find out, Mr. Cross, and how did you know we knew about Mrs. Wheeling?"

"When you were questioning me the first time I saw the file with Trinity's name on it; I hadn't heard from her in while, and just figured her husband either found out or that she was trying to work on her marriage. It wasn't until I got home that I remembered the news report about the Colorado businesswoman being found dead and I just kind of put it all together. I didn't want to believe it, but I did a bit of a search and found her obituary. I wanted to but didn't think that it was appropriate to call her husband and offer my condolences."

Marcum glanced back at the captain and he nodded letting her know that he believed the man's story. As he turned back to face Graylin, he watched in silence as the man wiped his eyes of the tears that were slowly building.

"I'm sorry, Mr. Cross," his voice softened, "but, how do you know that Elise went to Denver and met with Mrs. Grey? Did Elise tell you?"

"No," Graylin looked up, "one thing I do know about my ex-wife is that she's not stupid. Trinity actually called me when Elise had left her office and she told me about the conversation. What was interesting is that Trinity warned me about Elise, she told me that she was obsessed with me; she even told me that I need to get my phone and my laptop checked for spyware."

"What do you think, Mr. Cross?" Rowlings asked.

Graylin sat back thinking. All of the shit they'd been through during their marriage; all of their arguments started after days upon days of silence and they would finally spark with her accusing him of talking to other women. She was extremely jealous, and he'd never really thought about that until this moment. As a writer, he was used to his female fans and had come to love them as fans; but as he thought about it now, he could remember the looks that Elise would give any a hug or beg for his autograph.

"Damn," he whispered. "I never really paid it any mind. I just thought that she was a jealous woman. I mean, she met me on one of my book tours and she seen how my fans are."

"What are you thinking, Mr. Cross?"

"We argued a lot, and I do mean a lot. It was when we argued that I'd learn new shit about her and I always thought that was strange."

"Such as?" Rowlings asked.

"She was supposedly abused as a girl by a teacher," Graylin was rubbing his temples. "That's how I found out about her parents being dead and being raised by her grandmother, but she would never tell me any of their names... just that she was alone except for me. She also told me once that she'd been on the streets and even sold herself because of a man...

"A man that she'd been with." Graylin jumped from the seat feeling stupid. "For a goddamn writer... I missed everything."

Time after time Elise had lashed out at him, and more times than not he was the insensitive one. Monster, she would call him, and she'd tell him that he was cold and cruel. He couldn't count the number of times she'd accused him of being with another woman. He'd always just let it go, maybe call her crazy under his breath, but now he was beginning to see that his wife really was crazy.

"What do you think happened to this other man?" he finally asked.

"Let me ask you this," Marcum had returned to the edge of the desk, "are you sure that you didn't know her before you initially met her?"

"Not that I know of," Graylin searched his memories for anything even remote resembling Elise in his past. "Why? Did you find something?"

"We found an old website called Cross Super Fan, and even though the name is different, we're almost positive that it was her; the username on the account was daemon cross. Do you recognize it?"

"Daemon Cross?" Graylin felt like he'd turned two shades of white and was sure he looked as if he'd seen a ghost. He dropped his head into his hands and sat there rubbing it with the tips of his fingers. "Are you sure that it was Daemon Cross?"

"Positive, what's wrong?" Abraham stepped forward.

"Shortly after my little girl's mom and I broke up the first time, I joined this online group. It was a little different than Facebook is now, but it was very similar. It was a social built around role playing from games to… sex. I was just getting back into my writing and I was using this medium as my muse of a sorts to write out some of the erotica stuff I was exploring in my stories. I met a female submissive there by the name of daemon cross shortly after I joined. Goddamn, this is like ten years ago."

"How did that online relationship end?" Marcum asked.

"Not good," Graylin shook his head. "Things I was being told just didn't jive if I remember right and I uncollared her and told her that we could no longer talk. In the months that we played online I never talked to her on the phone, for me it was all fantasy because Sadè and I were trying to work things out. There were too many times she had me thinking that she was taking things too serious."

"So, this obsession with you is something that's been building for years," Abraham stated the obvious. "Mr. Cross, did you tell her that you were a writer?"

"Back then I wasn't published, but she'd read some of the things I'd written because they were usually based on our playing. Look," Graylin was rubbing his temples again trying to abate the growing headache, "what does all of this mean? I need to know if you think that Elise killed her first husband, and you never told me what happened with her son. And, is she responsible for Trinity?"

"The little boy is with his father's people and he's safe," Abraham answered him. "I called and talked to the grandmother and the little boy is doing quite well."

One less thing to worry about, Graylin couldn't do anything except shake his head. All of this was entirely too much to deal with. His mind was rushing through a dozen scenarios all at one time, and it was nauseating his stomach to the point that felt the need to vomit. He'd set up a trust fund for the little boy and let his grandparents know about it once all of this other bullshit was taken care of. Right now, he needed to know Elise's endgame.

"Mr. Cross, we haven't asked but," Capt. Rowlings was staring into his eyes to the point it was making him nervous, "were you sleeping with Mrs. Grey?"

"Yes," he didn't hesitate to answer. "I wasn't with Elise and hadn't been for months before I even started taking to Trinity, but we'd been together a few times. I just don't know how Elise would have known."

"Because of the pure nicotine being the cause of death for the previous husband and Mrs. Wheeling we suspect Ms. Mannsen, but it's purely circumstantial as of now."

"What about the fact that she was in Denver?" Graylin was confused and angry; to him as a writer, the police had more than enough to bring her ass in and question her.

"The hardest part about this is that we have nothing else, no fingerprints, no syringe or the vial with the nicotine. We've searched her home twice now and if we do anything further without more evidence that would be considered harassment."

Graylin was back up and pacing around the office. He could feel their eyes on him, but their assessment of him had changed drastically. "So, she was trying to pin her beating on me," he just stated out the blue, but he turned and stared at Marcum. "She was going to frame me for Trinity's death, wasn't she? That's what I would have done in my stories. The antagonist would have twisted everything until there was no way that I could prove that I was innocent."

"That's the path we were on until we confirmed that you were out of town," Marcum shrugged his shoulder. "She was so sure of herself until I asked her if she knew you had gone out of town at the time she was beaten, and of course her story changed just enough to take your name out of the equation."

"That explains the call the next morning." They were looking at him waiting for him to go into details. "She called me demanding to know where I'd been, and then just like always she began accusing me of sleeping with someone. I was actually away at a writers' convention in Atlanta."

"I'm afraid that you may be in danger, Mr. Cross," Capt. Rowlings informed him. "To be honest, we've never had to deal with a person so calculating, and like Det. Marcum said we cannot do anything without any concrete evidence. We brought you in today to let you know what is going on, and to warn you that she may be a very dangerous woman. So far, we know of at least two possible deaths she may be responsible for, but any woman you've been and you yourself could be a potential target."

"So, what do I do, huh? Do I run and hide, close up my house and become a recluse? I cannot let this woman hold this much power over me."

"We're really not sure what to tell you to do," Rowlings continued as Marcum and Abraham looked on. "All we can do at this time is let you know that we're still investigating her and the moment we find out anything I'll personally be in touch. I can offer police protection, but we're short staffed and that would mean I'd have to ask for volunteers to pull extra duties."

"No," Graylin shook his head. "I won't be a prisoner in my own goddamn home."

"What would you have us do?"

"Just find your evidence, Captain… please." Graylin was walking towards the door. "The funny part is, this entire thing is like a hellava plot for a crazy ass book that I just may have to write in the end."

His laughter wasn't real, but at this point all he wanted to do was get out into the air and clear his mind. The fact that Elise had found out about Trinity worried him. They'd been separated for almost a year now, but that hadn't stopped her from killing Trinity. He needed to get home and make a few cars to check on some people, and he needed to get a hold of his boy to come by and take a look at his computer.

"Damn… ain't all of this some shit?"

She'd been able to get away from home without her "keepers" realizing that she'd left. In Amelia's car and feeling camouflaged that's to the flowing traffic, Elise watched as Graylin walked out of the police station and towards his car. He'd been in there for almost two hours, and her curiosity was killing her to know why they'd called him in. She thumbed her phone giving thought to calling him just to hear his voice, but right now wouldn't be the best time for that.

"You go home for now, Baby," she blew him a kiss as his car pulled off into traffic, "and I'll talk to you in the morning."

Chapter 11: The Book Tour

The last time someone was beating at his door this hard and this insistent the police had slapped cuffs on him and drug him downtown because his ex-wife had told them that he'd beat her up. He was exhausted and trumped down the stairs in nothing more than his boxers and a robe rubbing at his temples trying to ease away the ever-present headache throbbing just below the surface.

"Stop banging on my fucking door," he shouted as he reached the floor. "I'm coming... shit."

Seeing Elise standing at his door with her hands on her hips, Graylin quickly cinched up his robe and stood there staring back down at her. "What do you want, Elise, and make it quick because I'm fucking tired."

His reflexes were not quick enough to stop the hand that suddenly struck his face, and Graylin couldn't do anything but stare at Elise as she stood there. "Where the fuck has you been, don't you know that I've been worried?"

His mouth dropped open as she moved up against his body and the same hand gently stroked the spot she'd just struck. His body was frozen in place as he watched her slap him again and again in his mind before the pain began to register. Her hand was soft and gentle, and the kiss to his cheek that followed was almost endearing, but the kiss to his lips woke him and brought his mind flying back to the present.

"What the fuck are you doing?" he pulled back from her. "Why are you here, Elise?"

"I came to check on my husband," she reached out trying to touch his face again, but he blocked her hand. "Where have you been, I've trying to get a hold of you for over two weeks."

"I had a tour out of the state for my new book, Elise, so I've been gone. You really need to go."

"Why didn't you answer your phone?" she was insisting on getting her answers. "I called you, I don't know how many times. I was afraid that something had happened to you."

"I didn't take my phone," he informed her. "I'd gotten some news that a really close friend of mine had passed away and I threw the damn thing against the wall."

Elise stared at him, her eyes unblinking looking deeply into his eyes trying to discern if he was telling her the truth. It was so unlike Graylin not to have his phone because all of his business contacts were stored in his phone, but him tossing it against the wall definitely sounded just like him.

"Why didn't you answer my instant messages?"

"Jacen has my laptop," he shrugged his shoulders. "I think I had a virus on it and he checked it out for me and then overnighted it to me while I was in Dallas."

"Dallas?" her eyebrow raised. "What were you doing in Dallas?"

"I told you, not that it's any of your business, but I was doing a tour and it took me through Dallas." Graylin watched as her facial expressions changed. He wanted to smile because she was aware who he was close to. "I was able to get a hold of LynMarie while I was there. I took her out to dinner and we talked for hours getting all caught up."

"Fuck you, Graylin," Elise hissed. "I've been here worried as shit over your ass and you was out having dinner with that little bitch."

"Amazing how she's a bitch now, but she wasn't one when you introduced her to me. What the fuck is your problem?"

"Forget it, Graylin," she stomped down the stairs and stormed off to her car.

Graylin smiled as he waved as she sped off in a ripping, screech of tire rubber.

"Fucking, crazy ass," he mumbled as he stepped back into his house and closed the door.

■■■■

"I was really surprised to hear that you were in town," the sound of her voice pulled his eyes away from the menu and look up. Graylin had to hold his breath as the pretty little girl he'd known stood before him as a beautiful woman. Gone was the shorter hair now replaced with curls and waves of brunette locks flowing past her shoulders towards the middle of her back. Heels.

"You're wearing heels," his first words rung in his head as being stupid.

"Yes, Sir," she was giggling, "I am. Very observant."

"Yea," Graylin laughed at himself before stepping around the table and pulling her into his arms. "It's been a long time, LynMarie, you look gorgeous."

"You look rather gorgeous yourself, um..."

"Say it," he smiled as he waited.

"Graylin." LynMarie couldn't help blushing; she'd rarely called him by his first name due to the nature of their relationship. "It's so good to see you. More than you'll ever know."

"I'm just glad you agreed to see me," he pulled out her chair waiting for her to sit. As he returned to his seat he waves for a waiter.

"Why wouldn't I see you?"

Graylin dropped his head as memories flooded his head. They hadn't talked in years because he thought it was best for her. Things with Elise were mountain sliding fast and he didn't was LynMarie caught up in things. He'd missed her. He'd missed everything about her, and to see her today. He looked up smiling.

"Graylin, I don't blame you like you think I do," LynMarie reached out taking his hand. "I was scared for you, and I wanted to be there for you. I wanted to be there with you."

"I was sure that you hated me," his chuckle was a nervous one. "Things just got so bad so fast and she was so goddamn erratic. So many threats and so many fights."

"You know I never hated her until it felt like she took you from me," it was LynMarie's turn to drop her head. Glancing up through her lashes she was greeted with a smile.

"She never took me from you, Angel," his pet name for her caused her cheeks to flame a rosy red. "I had to keep you safe. There was something different about Elise, and by the time I finally walked away your life had taken on to a new road. I didn't want to disrupt that by adding confusion."

"I've never been confused about, Sir," she blushed as he pressed his lips to her fingers. "There's no one that I'll ever love like you."

Her brown eyes glowed and he couldn't find anything false in what she'd said. Graylin was at a loss for words, but he knew he still cared immensely for this young lady. That night he'd shared her with Elise sparked a flame that burned so bright that his wife feared it eclipsed their marriage. She became jealous. She stomped around angry.

"I would never let her hurt you."

"I know, but I wanted to stay with you," there was a tear in the corners of her eyes as she stared at him.

"I know," he felt bad. He felt like he'd hurt her. "Enough of this, tell me something good."

The remainder of dinner was a flurry of traded stories filled with laughter as they got reacquainted. Graylin lauded the conversation with tales of his writing after he'd finally gotten his life. LynMarie surprised him by letting him know that she had all of his books and loved them. She told him about her husband and their very plain and simple life. He asked for details about her wedding day, and she gave him the fairy tale came true version.

Graylin wanted to be happy for her. He wanted her to be happy. LynMarie was describing how beautiful the wedding dress was, but there was something missing. Excitement. There was no enthusiasm in her voice. He listened not interrupting, smiling and nodding. But, for her it was just an act that he could tell she'd rehearsed and performed quite often.

He almost laughed, having forgotten that she definitely could talk once you got her to open up. Her voice was soft with a heavy, country twang that he used to love falling asleep listening to. She also has this cute little laugh that she would interject at times that always put a smile on his face. He'd missed talking to her. He missed a lot about her, and that repeated over and over in his head.

"Are you happy, LynMarie?" He interrupted her tale and watched her eyes.

LynMarie stared at him trying to maintain her smile. Her truth was simple, and it had been for the longest time. She was... content. Her husband was at good man. He was caring. Gentle. Endearing. He loved her with all of his heart and had told her so from day one. But, her heart was somewhere different. Her heart belonged to someone else all day it always had. She'd never stopped being in love with Graylin, and she'd never lied to herself about him.

"Yes, Sir," the words slipped from her lips as her eyes were cast down away from his. She grabbed her glass of wine sipping and hoping he'd believed her.

"Good," Graylin allowed her that lie for the moment. "That's all I ever wanted for you."

The awkward silence that followed was broken by his phone ringing. Pulling the cell from his jacket pocket he glanced at the screen and shook his head before answering. "Hello, Aura."

He sat staring across the table as LynMarie sipped at her wine watching him over the rim of her glass. Her eyes reminded him of the first time he'd seen her; opening the front door and she and Elise were both kneeling. It was the first time in a long time that he'd thought of his wife as beautiful, but that day they both were. They were wearing matching teddies that hung from their shoulders teasing him of what lie beneath the lacy fabric. That first time she glanced up welcoming him home... he fell in love with her eyes.

"Listen," he stopped Aura before she got started with his schedule for the next few days, "I can't talk right now. I'll call you tomorrow and we can go over things then."

LynMarie smiled listening to him as he spoke to his publicist. Elise hated that woman, making her appreciate Aura and the things she's done to help her Graylin get to where he was. She could hear him trying to talk his way out of their conversation. *No, Aura, I'm kinda busy right now...* She wanted to laugh at him as he waved at her to make certain she understood he was trying to get her off the phone. *We... Aura, we....*

"It's ok, Graylin," she winked at him as he shook his head.

"Look, Aura," he stopped the woman in mid-sentence, "I'm at dinner right night with someone very important, and we're getting caught up. I'll give you a call tomorrow, ok.

"No, Aura, she's not anyone that you know," he paused shrugging his shoulders and mouthing I'm sorry. "Like I said, I'll call you tomorrow, but tonight I'm all hers and it's been a long time since we've talked so there's a lot to catch up on. You have a good night."

Graylin hung up before Aura had a chance to say anything else. She'd have her ass on her shoulders tomorrow, but he was ok with that. He didn't know how much time he had with his angel, and he wasn't about to squander any of it talking and fussing with Aura.

"Sometimes she doesn't know when to just let it go," they both chuckled. "Like I told her, I'm all yours tonight. So, what would you like to do?"

"Can we..." she hesitated. "Can we get out of here and go to your hotel room?"

"Of course," Graylin was waving for the waitress as he pulled his wallet from his back pocket.

The walk from the hotel restaurant to the lobby elevator leading up to his suite was filled with them laughing and talking and holding hands like a couple of teens on a date to the prom. The more they talked, the more both realized that they were afraid they would never get to see the other again. Graylin couldn't take his eyes off her and as they walked her body pressed into his side making it hard for him to concentrate.

The few people who happened to be in the elevator with them most likely thought that they were a couple of newlyweds away from their family enjoying a small honeymoon. His arm was about her shoulders and hers around his waist. They were giggling and sharing whispers without a care for who was around them. The elevator rides up was probably the most fun that either of them had had in years, and the fact that they were together only made it that much better. At last the doors opened and Graylin led her off through the small gathering of people onto his suite door. They were almost running down the hall to his door, and the laughing hadn't ceased yet.

"Are you sure?" Graylin had stopped in front of a door and turned to look her in the eyes. "I mean… what about?"

With a finger she silenced him. Standing on her toes she kissed his lips softly. "I don't want to think about him. I want to concentrate on you."

The door opened into a dark living room as held her hand pulling her inside. Their eyes met as Graylin wrapped his arms around her waist, and she draped hers over his shoulders. For the few months they were shared with by Elise they'd never spent any time alone. Graylin had been accused several times that they had as her jealousy of the close bond he and LynMarie had formed in such a short time grew.

"I've always wished that she would have allowed me one night alone with you," LynMarie smiled up at him. "I never understood why she just started hating me."

"You were supposed to be hers and shared with me," Graylin leaned down to kiss her lips. "You were never supposed to get close to me. To this day I think it would eat her up to know that we're still close."

"Not just close, Sir," her voice softened. "Graylin, I have always and will always be in love with you."

"I know, Angel," he kissed her forehead. "And I'll always be in love with you. I guess that's why I was surprised that you'd meet me tonight."

"Why? Because of Michael?"

"You know me, I don't want to add to any confusion."

"Well, using what you'd said to Aura," she pulled his head down until their lips were just barely apart, "I'm all yours tonight."

The kiss began slowly with tentative pecks that grew into a passionate lock of their lips. Graylin groaned into her mouth as her fingernails gently bit into the back of his head. His hands roamed her spine as their feet shuffled across the floor. The stop was abrupt and LynMarie moaned as her back pressed against a wall. She was trapped, and his kiss became harder. Her body melted into his.

Graylin slowly slid a hand up her body starting at her hip. The dress just seemed to mold itself to her frame offering little resistance to his fingers. His pelvis kept her firmly pinned to the wall as he pressed his hand against her breast and squeezed. It was bare beneath the cotton of the dress. Her nipple was quick to respond to his touch, hardening and poking his palm as if begging for his attention. He could feel her vibrating, shivering against him. He traced her nipple through the dress and smiled as she pulled away from his lips to suck in a deep breath. His circles ended with him gently pinching and her gasping.

"You've always known just what to do or say to make my body respond to you," her eyes fluttered. Licking her lips, LynMarie pressed back into the wall watching him tease one nipple and then the other. Her nipples were already sensitive, but Graylin had her wishing he'd pull off her dress so the fabric wouldn't drag over them.

"I think your body has always known that you're mine," Graylin had leaned in to whisper into her ear. "Always known that you belong to me."

"Yes," her voice trembled.

Anticipation sent goosebumps up and down her arms and legs the moment his free hand began drifting down the side of her leg towards the hem of her dress. She was staring into his dark brown eyes and bit down on her bottom lip when she felt his fingers graze her bare thigh.

"You've always loved torturing me, Sir," she mumbled.

"It's the torture that makes the need taste so good," Graylin flashed his smile and squeezed at her inner thigh. "Watching that need turn to hunger... want... desires, and finally hearing you beg all of it just makes me smile."

LynMarie's eyes glazed over and slowly closed. The heat boiling across her entire body was more intense than anything she'd ever experienced, and she welcomed it. His fingers were playing soft notes to an unheard song against her inner thighs slowly making their way up the keys until the one thing she'd always wanted happened. She finally had the man she's always wanted all to herself. Her legs bowed open allowing him free access. Her breathing felt constricted as her throat tightened. Her lungs were burning before she realized that she was holding her breath, and she slowly released it. Her eyes fluttered opened to stare into his. His fingers reached her lips gently pressing inward.

"Please, please, Sir," she pulled his ear to her lips. "I need you, Graylin. Take what has always belonged to you. Please."

Their clothes disappeared in a furry of hands snatching and pulling away fabric. He kept her pressed to the wall his fingers tracing over the naked body that he'd seen in a countless number of dreams. From her neck down to her breasts, watching as the goosebumps prickled her flesh. Her nipples stood out and he gently pulled them. Her moans thrilled him. She was holding back, and he wanted so much more. He leaned forward sliding his tongue up and over her breast before sucking down upon the stiffened nipple.

"Oh my god," she mewled.

His teeth scraped across the sensitive piece of flesh before he bit down. Her hand was behind his head holding him in place as he sucked the tip of her breast into his mouth. Her moans were louder, and her body was shivering. In his head her eyes were closed, and her toes were curled up into the plush carpeting and he smiled. His hands dropped reaching behind her to squeeze on her ass, and his painfully hardened dick pressed into her belly. He was holding her tightly to his body.

"You're killing me," she kept murmuring.

"Tell me…" his breathing was heavy and his hand between her spread thighs was the only thing holding her up against the wall. His fingers were thrusting, churning her insides and she was vibrating against his palm. "Tell me now."

"Inside, Graylin," she was begging.

Her legs were pulled up onto his arms. Her back slid up the wall, and she moaned out again as his tongue started at her bellybutton and slowly moved up her abdomen back to her chest and she was slowly lowered. Her hands were holding his head and her fingernails were gently pressing into scalp. She bit down so hard on her bottom lip that there was the slight tinge of blood on her tongue. Her mouth fell open in a silent scream as he slowly eased his way into her craving body.

She felt him gently pressing forward, splitting her open slowly. His length eased inward and her ass was seated in his hands as he lowered her down until their eyes met. Her brown eyes met his brown eyes and the feelings that had been there years ago still burned just a brightly. Their lips met as he began to grind her back into the wall. She could feel him deep enough to swear he was in her belly and she wanted to beg for more. As he pulled back, her eyes stretched, and she moaned into his mouth as he filled her once again.

"Thank you, Sir," she mumbled over again and again as they moved together. "I love you, Graylin."

"I love you too…"

Chapter 12: "He Should Have Told Me."

"Good morning, Babe," her voice woke him, and he groaned regretting answering the phone.

"Why are you calling me, Elise?" Graylin grumbled into his cell phone. He was hoping that it was LynMarie calling to say good morning but hearing his ex-wife on the phone had his day already off on the wrong foot. "I had a late-night writing and I wanted to sleep in for a while."

"I won't keep you," her voice was too cheery after the talk they'd had just a couple of days before. "I just needed to hear your voice and to check up on you."

"I don't need you to keep tabs on me, Elise."

"You don't have to be mean, Graylin," she sounded hurt.

"I'm not being mean," he was biting his tongue. "Look, Elise, I just need some space. I really need for you to just let this go."

"You talk as if we aren't still married, Graylin," he could hear the tinge of frustration in her voice. "I am still your wife, and I still love you."

"Love me?" Aggravated, Graylin sat up in bed. He'd been wondering how to approach Elise with some of the information he'd gotten from the cops. Part of him wanted to know more about this dead husband and the child. The other part was under the impression that the cops were using him as a pawn; because that's how he would write it. That was a lot of information for them to pass on.

She was prattling on about nothing as if he was paying attention. His mind was lost on a million other things at one time including the research he'd been doing into his past with her. Somewhere they'd crossed paths before the bookstore, but where? Through whom? Why? So many more questions than answers, and he knew she'd not answer any of them.

"Damn," it came out louder than he wanted.

"Did you hear me, Graylin?" Her voice rattled in his ear.

"To be honest," he took a deep breath, "no I didn't, Elise. What did you say?"

"Who was that little girl you had a few days ago?"

"Wait... huh?" That had his full attention. He replayed the question in his head a few times before he could think of a response. "What are you talking about, Elise?"

"Don't play stupid with me," she sounded perturbed. "Who was she?"

"Elise," Graylin had to fight to remain calm, "how do you know I had a little girl with me a few days ago?"

"How is not important or the goddamn question, Graylin," now she was angry, and he could hear. That's the Elise that he knew well.

"That is the goddamn question," matching her tone. "Are you fucking following me? No, wait... don't even answer because I don't give a fuck."

"You don't give a fuck?" Her words were venom dripping into his ear. "A child and a woman. Who is the woman, Graylin, and why were you at her house?"

"It's none of your goddamn business, Elise," his words were spit through ground teeth. He was now sitting on the edge of his bed wondering if he was overreacting, but the truth was... she was either watching him or she had someone doing it for her.

"We're still married..." she quickly punched in.

"Look for those papers soon, Elise," Graylin drew in a deep breath to calm his words and his nerves.

"You should have told me about the little girl, Graylin," he could hear her crying. "Why wouldn't you tell me something like that? I don't... I don't understand."

"I'm done with this and I'm done with you." Graylin was no longer interested in hearing anything else that she had to say. It was past time for him to push her completely away and move on with his life. "Don't call this number anymore because I won't answer. Good bye."

Elise couldn't move. The phone was still pressed to her ear and she was listening to the silence. He'd hung up. He'd told her good bye and hung up on her. She could feel the heat building, first just below her ears and flowing outward through her entire body. All she could see was red... before she exploded.

The phone crashed and splintered against the wall. She felt her throat vibrating, but she never heard the scream that vibrated through the room. Her stomach churned, she couldn't shake the sound of his words rattling around in her head. The anger was making her feel ill, but she swarmed around the bedroom ripping apart anything that wasn't nailed down.

"Who do you think you are?" She shrieked as she ripped the curtains from the wall. A lamp flew across the room and shattered. "I hate you. I fucking hate you, you bastard."

Her heart was pounding in her chest sounding like a hollow drum in her ears. Her breathing was shallow, and her arms felt heavy. She stood on shaky legs staring at the small table gripped tightly in her hands. Tears were streaming from her eyes clouding her vision as she dropped the table was sunk to her knees. Elise slumped down into the carpet crying and gasping for air. She felt... broken. Betrayed. She was angry.

"You're going to hurt," she'd sat up staring about the torn room. "You're going to pay dearly, Graylin Cross, I promise you that."

Aura slowly walked into the bedroom, she'd been in the hall listening to get heated conversation between Graylin and Elise. She'd trying to be supportive where that woman was concerned, but since that day in the book store she hadn't cared for her. There was just something about Elise that didn't sit right with her, and the way it always left Graylin...

He was still on the edge of the bed with his head dropped. He hadn't seen her walk in and jumped as she began gently massaging his temples. She'd often wondered what he'd think or say if she told him her true feelings. They'd been working together for a few years, and it was getting harder to contain that she was in love with him. Even now, nursing him as he was brooding over that bitch, Aura was content. She felt that it was her place to be at his side.

"What did she do this time?" Her voice was the exact opposite of what he'd just been dealing with. Aura always had a way of calming him. Soothing his brain. She knew of to get him back in focus, and he truly appreciated that of her.

"I think she's stalking me." To even hear the works, it sounded crazy. He'd written about stalkers and killers, but that was just sick fantasy for him. Why would anyone, especially his ex-wife, want to follow him around?

"What do you mean, stalking you?" She sounded confused, but nothing about Elise shocked or confounded her. As far as she was concerned, Elise Mannsen was certifiable.

"She asked me about Kennadey and her mom."

"You never told her about Sadè?" That surprised her.

"No," Graylin shook his head. "I never got around to it, and then we started having all of the arguments and shit. I didn't want Kenni around that, and to be honest, Aura, I didn't trust her."

"Well you know how I feel about her crazy ass." Aura laughed hoping he'd join in.

"Goddamn," Graylin groaned, "what the fuck did I do in my past life to have to go through this shit? This woman is going to be the death of me."

Dropping to her knees and lifting his head up to look into his eyes, Aura smiled. Graylin smiled back as her sparkling green eyes hypnotic spell worked their magic in relaxing him. He sat there taking her in kneeling with year hem of the short dress sliding up on her thighs giving him a lot to appreciate. The neckline of the dress was cut low offering him a deep look into her cleavage and wondering if she was wearing a bra. If he were to guess, from the way her full buxom lay on her chest, he'd say no.

"You're such a tease," he looked up into her eyes.

"What?" Her giggle was infectious and what he needed. "What I do now?"

Their relationship blurred all of the lines between them. She hadn't said it, because between them there were supposed to be "No strings attached ", but he knew that Aura was in love with him. He had feelings for her, cared for her, but with all of the shit going on around him he just didn't want to be "in love" with anybody. They were around great pair, they worked well together, but right now he needed his room.

"This right here," he reached out cupping his hands over her breasts confirming that she wasn't wearing a bra.

"And how is that teasing you?" Aura took a deep breath trying to steady her excitement. He would often try to fight his urges to have her, and she was quick to remind him that there was nothing to worry about. But, each time he touched her the flames of her desires for him only burned brighter. Her nipples hardened beneath his hands and her dress causing her to moan softly.

"You love teasing me," he squeezed, and Aura's closed eyes tightened, and her breathing gurgled softly through partially parted lips. He slid his hands up to the tops of her breasts and slipped beneath the fabric to palm her bare flesh.

"Now who's teasing whom, Mr. Cross?" Her hazy eyes opened, and she bit down on her bottom lip.

His hands were warm but felt cool against her heated body. The second his hands grazed her nipples she moaned out and sat up on her knees wrapping her arms around his neck. Their lips met. The kiss felt like it was searing her lips, and she opened her mouth inviting his tongue in. Graylin was never one to disappoint, slipping his long tongue into her mouth to playfully spar with her own. There was always something so passionate and attentive about the way he kissed her; she'd almost swear he cared for her as strongly as she cared for him.

His fingers lightly pinched her nipples drawing out a moan that echoed in their conjoined mouths. Pressing his hands down the dress complied with his demands sliding over her breasts and down her arms. The cool air of his room caused goosebumps to pop up all over exposed flesh. Pulling away from her mouth Graylin leaned forward and traced his tongue around her nipple before drawing it into his mouth and sucking… hard. His teeth grazed and bit down eliciting the near scream he'd been waiting for.

"I'd say I'm doing more than just teasing," he drew in a deep breath and licked his lips as he helped her to stand.

The dress clung to her body. Graylin tugged watching as it slid down past her belly exposing her bellybutton. He traced his tongue down from between her breasts to swirl around the edge of her navel, and her giggling made her abdomen undulate. The dress was sliding over her hips exposing the satiny thong beneath. The dress dropped to the floor around her bare feet, and he looked up at her smiling.

Aura could barely contain herself as Graylin removed her dress. She loved the attention he'd pay to her body; kissing every part of her as the dress slid away. Her heart was pounding; she could hear it between her ears mixing with her quickened breathing. Her toes were curling into the soft, plush carpet that Graylin had opted to have in his bedroom, and her fingers were clinched into his shoulders.

His tongue was like liquid fire burning down her body. Starting at her nipples, so hard that they hurt, and all over her breasts; on down her belly and to her navel where he swirled just the tip around just enough to tickle her flesh. His hands were on her butt squeezing at her cheeks as he kissed at the front of her panties causing her knees to wobble just a little. His tongue slid up the inside of her thigh and she almost screamed.

"You're so not right, Graylin," she panted. Her hands were on the top of his head as he pressed his face between her thighs and she felt his tongue teasing her through what little fabric covered her. Her legs parted around his face allowing him more space to move around, and she was rewarded with his tongue pressing its way around her panties.

Graylin hooked his thumbs into the slender waistband of her panties pulling them down as he dropped to his knees in front of her. Once they were over her hips and out of his way, he pressed his lingual attack between her silken legs. Her body trembled over him and he could feel her stretching up on her toes and holding on to his head to keep from falling over. His tongue was everywhere at once and her body responded accordingly with muscles twitching and contracting and the sounds of her moans bouncing from the walls until she begged him to…

"Stop, please, Graylin. No more."

Slipping from between her thighs, he stood removing his own clothing. He grinned as she stood there waving about on shaky legs and he wondered if she would fall if left standing much longer. Stepping up behind her, Graylin pressed his body against hers and she shivered. His hands were at her waist and he was pushing her forward towards his bed.

No words were spoken as she was pushed up on the bed on her stomach and then turned her over onto her back. Her legs fell open to him and their bodies slowly began to melt together as he crawled between her spread thighs until he was looking down into her face. He was more than ready for her, and from the heat scorching at his legs, she was more than ready for him. With a grunt he eased his way into her as her fingers clawed at his arms.

His thrusts were slow and building. Her eyes were rolled back in her head. Her breathing was rushed and shallow as she held on to her lover while he took his passionate needs out on her willing body. Her moans were loud and ringing in his ears as he leaned over her body filling her with each stroke. As cool as he kept his bedroom, he couldn't only feel the heat that their bodies generated being cooled slightly by the sweat dripping from his down onto hers.

Aura was tossing her head. Her body was on fire and Graylin was feeding the flames stroke after stroke. Their lips met, and he was grinding and gyrating down into her. Her legs were wrapped around his waist locking him in. She was chanting his name and he was biting at her neck as their bodies moved together.

"Oh my god, Graylin," she was almost screeching, "I love you."

Everything stopped.

Elise was staring at what remained of her cell phone lying on the floor in pieces. Before she'd called him, she'd been going through her emails, and it was one that she'd seen that prompted the call. There hadn't been a return email address, but it was clearly for her and contained an mp3 attachment. As she listened, her entire world felt as if it crashed in on her.

Hello, Elise, the voice was distorted so she couldn't tell if it was a male or female's. *Yes, I know you more than you'd think. I know of your past and that you were once married and that you have a little boy who has never seen you. I know that your husband died, and that you had been a primary suspect. I know that you've been stalking your ex-husband... what are you looking for? Maybe I can help you, and all that I want in return is absolutely... Nothing.*

The red-haired slut is going to his house right now and she's dressed to kill. What will you do, Elise? Will you just sit here, or will you go over there? There's a key to the front door under the potter.

Elise had been sitting in her car outside of Graylin' house once again. She couldn't help herself because in her mind she was still in love with this man who was making it pretty clear that he no longer wanted her. Their phone call not even an hour ago was proof positive that he wanted to move forward without her, but she had to find a way to prove to him that he needed her. But, that damn email had her rattled.

Aura's bright, yellow BMW was sitting in his driveway. Elise shook her head. Who in the hell would want a bright yellow car of any kind?

"What the fuck are you doing here, Bitch?" she hissed looking around to see if there was anyone out who would recognize her. She'd been over there, and they'd had too many confrontations in the front of his house that if she were seen the police would most likely be called.

Stepping from her car, Elise casually walked up to the front door and tipped the potter over. The key was there as promised, and she used it to unlock the door and slipping into Graylin' home. She quietly closed the door before removed her shoes. She'd only been inside once before, and he'd made changes since then, but it was so beautiful. She could almost smell a woman's hand in decorating because Graylin was never any good at that, and it was most likely that little red-haired slut.

The sounds of the two of them just seemed to fill every room in the house, and she stood there listening. Her stomach felt as if it was lodged in her throat and her eyes burned with tears. In her mind she could see them rutting around on his bed like a couple of animals, and it destroyed her over and over each time she screamed out. In the years that she'd been with him, Graylin had never made her scream; there'd been passion, but the way Aura was calling out his name it was like he was fucking her like a god.

Elise was jealous, and then her whole world stopped suddenly when Aura screamed out one last time.

"*Oh my god, Graylin, I love you.*"

Elise fled from the house not bothering to close up as she left.

Chapter 13: The Pawns are in Place

Aura sat on her sofa feeling refreshed and comfortable. She'd left Graylin still in bed sleeping like a baby and came home to shower and reap the rewards of her game. She teased herself with the word "game" but it was so much more than that. Everything that she was doing has taken years to put into place, and now she was finally ready to push the envelope. Now it was time to push everything to the edge.

She settled back into the sofa placing her laptop on the cushion beside her. Her skin was a little flush from the hot shower, but she was lounging in her favorite comfy attire of a bra, panties and knee-high socks; all matching of course. She'd almost gotten a ticket racing to get home to view the recording on her computer, but the cop was feeling generous. Now she was ready. The stage was set, and she was prepared for something... beautiful.

Elise Mannsen, that wasn't even her real name. If Graylin knew half as much about this woman as she knew he would have never married her. Aura had tried to talk to him about her, but every conversation seemed to get pushed around to her acting like a jealous side chick; she was not jealous. She'd made a pact with him that there would be no strings attached, but that didn't mean she wouldn't look out for his best interests. After all of the bullshit he has to go through dealing with Sadè, the last thing she'd wanted was someone like Elise in his life.

She'd paid a lot of money to have this woman's past dug up. She's quite the enigma. The name she uses now, she'd changed it to after the death of her first husband. The child she had, that only a select few knew about, now lives with her ex-in-laws. There were the criminal charges hanging over her head surrounding her first husband's death; now that was something that she knew more about than anyone. She no longer needed a picture to see the face of the one woman she'd grown to hate. Closing her eyes and Elise stood before her dressed in all of the lies of her past. Gone were the dead parents who died when she was all little girl; the grandmother who never raised her; the life she never had. Her real life replaced by a childhood in and out of foster homes; being a runaway and living on the streets; and even a time of prostitution and drugs.

"I know you quite well, little liar." Aura opened her eyes smiling; having the upper hand was one thing, and she loved knowing more than most. Using what she knew kept her several steps ahead of everyone, and that's what she preferred.

Graylin would know everything soon enough, and he'd thank her. No... he would love her. He would finally have his eyes open and see that she was best for him. That she could and would protect him. That she was the only woman; good enough, strong enough to love him right.

"So," she pulled the laptop onto her lap and pulled open the top, "let's see what we have here, shall we."

Finding the video, she'd recorded at Graylin house, Aura found herself smiling from ear to ear. It had played out just as she'd seen it all in her head. The seduction of Graylin was always a treat because, quite frankly, the man knew just how to satisfy her in ways no other man has ever been able to. But, what made that entire moment sweeter was the look on Elise's face the moment she screamed out to Graylin that she loved him. It was all planned right down to the very second, and thanks to a few things she'd set up to know just when Elise had walked into the house.

From the moment she'd sent Elise the text that the red head woman; meaning herself, was at Graylin' house to the moment that Elise walked into the house she knew exactly what she wanted to happen. She was the puppeteer, and they were all her little dolls moving in a choreographed dance at her whim. She wanted to get up and dance around the living room but opted to sit there and watch the video over and over just to study the look on Elise's face.

Grunting and pausing the video Aura picked up her ringing phone and glanced at the screen to see who was calling. "Damn," she mumbled before answering. "Hello, Ms. Rivers."

"Hey Aura," Mishelle was all business, "I just wanted to check on the schedule of our boy for the next few weeks. I need him to come up here to sit with a screenwriter so that we can get a few new projects up and running."

"Give me a moment to grab the day planner and I can give you a full rundown," she was shaking her head because this was her off day. "I don't believe he's changed anything."

"Changed as in?"

"He's gotten to where he loves to take these little side trips off schedule," Aura explained, "but it looks as if things are on track for the next few weeks. There's not a whole lot on the itinerary. He's scheduled to get a lot of writing done because he has that deadline with you on the twenty-third. We do have a complete opening next week for a few days where I could get him up to you."

"That would work out perfectly," Mishelle answered. "You get him up here during those three days and I can make good use of all three. He needs a new portfolio picture taken so I can get him in with a photographer, and we can get a few radio spots done with a DJ I know here as well as some commercial spots done."

"Sounds like a plan, Ms. Rivers," Aura smiled. "I'll get with Mr. Cross today and let him know what all you have in mind and I'll get the ticket taken care of. Anything else, Ma'am?"

"No," Mishelle was slow to answer. There was something going on that she was not being told. She could feel it and figured she'd just discuss it with Graylin when he got to town, but in the back of her mind she was having a hard time with this woman now. "No, just get that taken care of and tell Graylin that I'll see him in a few days and come ready to work."

"I sure will."

Hanging up the phone Aura sat there for a moment. Mishelle Rivers was a very astute woman, and for a moment she wondered what could have caused her to pause like that. Thinking through their conversation she couldn't think of anything that would cause any kind of worry or confusion, but that doesn't mean that Mishelle didn't catch something. She'd have to be more careful from this point on because all it would take was a word and Graylin would drop her in a heartbeat. She needed to cement herself into his life and soon.

■■■■

Elise couldn't move. Her body refused to listen, not that she had anything to tell it. She'd made it as far as her sofa and that's where she'd stopped. Her mind was replaying the words she'd heard while standing in his house, and it wouldn't stop. The sofa cushion was soaked; she'd cried all night until she just had no more tears. Her heart ached, and her body felt numb.

"How could you, Graylin?" she'd heard those words from her mouth since she'd walked out of his house.

Sharp pains stormed through her head trapping her in the darkness of her mind trying to deal with the contractions. She could hear her blood rushing through her veins and her heart was like a bass drum pounding between her ears. Her stomach was lurching and at times she could taste the bile boiling over. Her eyes were closed trying to block out the images of what she hadn't seen but heard. She could picture him coupled with that... that woman, grunting and groaning and rutting like animals. She could imagine him between her spread thighs and Aura's fingernails scratching into his back as he thrusts drove her down into his mattress. And then the words screamed out, it's as if Aura had known she was standing downstairs listening.

"Oh my god, Graylin, I love you."

"Why," she murmured. "Why, you son-of-a-bitch? How could you betray me like that?"

Elise forced her body to sit up and she wiped away the tears that covered her face. Her eyes felt swollen, and her lip hurt from where she'd been biting on it. Her head was swimming and for a moment nothing around her looked familiar. Shaking her head to clear the cobwebs and she opened her eyes slowly to look around once more. The place where she was sitting was her living room, but it was the living room from a past she'd walked away from and thought to never revisit.

Standing, she slowly moved around the house turning up her nose. The sofa was old, a hand-me-down from her neighbors because they were getting new furniture and her husband thought it was good to accept the piece of trash. She stopped. Her husband wasn't Graylin, it was...

"Goddamn, Elise," Terrence walked through the backdoor of the modest sized, double wide trailer staring at her. His eyes were bloodshot red and that meant he'd been smoking weed again with the neighbor, and even from the door his breath smelled of beer. "What the fuck are you doing? Why aren't you cooking dinner yet?"

"What the fuck have you been doing all day, Terrence? I've been working, so why haven't you started cooking?"

This was just one of a million different arguments that they had daily. The only thing she could depend on was that he was never violent. He was a very stupid drunk; he'd smoke, drink, come home fuss for a moment and she'd have to drag his sorry ass to the bedroom where he could sleep it off.

He walked up on her causing her to step back as he stumbled. Once upon a time there was a moment that she actually had feelings for him, but since the baby she felt nothing for him. The only good thing about Terrence Kaine was that he resembled the one man that she was desperately in love with; Graylin Cross. There was just something beautiful about that man, and she knew more about him than she knew about her own husband.

"You're such a sad bitch," Terrence was so close that she could feel the heat of his breath on her face. She wrinkled her nose wanting to walk away, but he'd walked her into a wall in the kitchen trapping her. His words alone made him mean, and she hated him and often wished him dead. "I don't know why I keep your ass around… it's not like I get any pussy from you anymore. Had that goddamn kid and now the fuckin' shop is closed to a nigga. What the fuck?"

"You don't deserve anything from me, Terrence," she pushed at his forehead hoping to move his face from being directly in front of her own. "Why don't you just leave? I wouldn't stop you. It's not like you help me around here."

Elise realized that she hadn't moved. She was still standing back near the sofa watching all of this unfold right before her eyes. Her life was haunting her. It was a part of her past that she hadn't thought about in years, and now here it was. It felt like she could reach out and touch Terrence and herself; it all looked so real. This was the last time she'd seen her first husband alive. She would eventually have to help him to their bedroom where he'd pass out. She would sleep on the sofa that night and when she'd wake up in the morning she would find Terrence still in the bed and she would leave for work. It would be when she got home from work that the drama would start.

She sat back down on the sofa as they continued arguing. His words were like knives stabbing her in the heart and with each she began to see him stretched out before her dead. He was the worse person she'd ever allowed into her life. Even living on the streets and selling her body she never felt this bad about herself. Terrence had a way of making her feel like shit. She'd gone to sleep that night begging for him to just never wake up, and she'd later find out that's exactly what happened.

When she got home that night after work the police was at her home. Her in-laws and the paramedics were there as well. His mother had walked up to her and slapped her so hard that she'd seen stars, and the woman swore that she would make certain that she would be held responsible.

"What's going on?" she'd found the babysitter just before the police had pulled her aside to talk to her.

"I came over to drop the baby off with Terrence," the young girl began, "and when he wouldn't answer I let myself in with the key you'd given me. I didn't want to go into your room, but he wasn't answering me, so I went in to check on him and well…"

"Well?"

"He's dead."

A wish... a dream answered.

Elise sat up on the sofa and looked around. The living room swam before her eyes for a moment before clearing. Her stomach rolled and growled but quickly settled. She brushed her hair back from her eyes and drew in a few deep breaths. She was no longer looking back on that night and yet the feeling was still there hanging thickly in the air around her. Everything was so different from that time and yet it was all so very familiar. The hate had returned. It was to so heavy that it made her body hurt.

She stood on shaky legs. Her balance was tested as she moved from the living room and into the kitchen. Her steps were slow, but she made it in there and started her some coffee. As that was being prepared, she moved upstairs and into her bedroom. She wanted to take a shower just to wash away the feeling that was consuming her. The house phone was lying on the bed. The voices in her head were screaming for her not to do what she'd done so naturally since they day they split up, and she refused to listen.

As the phone rang, Elise removed her clothing. She needed him to pick up the phone... she needed him to answer her call.

"Hello," his voice always managed to soothe her, especially that low growl when he first woke up. "Elise, I know it's you. Elise?"

"Hi, Baby," she spoke softly not wanting to wake him completely. "I know you said not to call, but I needed to hear your voice."

"Are you, all right?" he sounded concerned. "What's going on?"

"Graylin," her voice was shaky as she spoke his name. "I just want you to know... I need you to know..."

"What? What's wrong, Elise?"

She stood there naked and crying holding on to the phone with both hands. She wanted to hate him. She wanted to scream out and call him all of the things she'd call Terrence, but the words stuck in her throat.

Elise?"

"I'm sorry, Baby," she was sniffling. "I'm so sorry for all of the shit I've done and said. I know that you cannot forgive me right now, but you have to believe me. I need you know that I love you, Graylin. I love you beyond words.

"You have to believe me..." Elise hung up the phone.

Her knees buckled dropping her to the floor and the tears started falling once again. She wanted to scream, but she didn't have the strength to do any more than sob pitifully on her bedroom floor. She couldn't stop herself from beating her head into the carpeting until she felt dizzy lying there.

Drawing her knees under her body she slowly picked herself up from the floor. Her head was hurting now, and her eyes were glazed. She walked back to the bed and sat down, and it was at this point she noticed the folded piece of paper. She had no desire to read it, but her fingers fumbled with the edges until it opened, and she was staring at the words.

Must you always let a man make you weak? You're probably lying around crying after hearing the two of them together when you should be plotting to get even. You should want him to hurt and yet knowing you, Elise, you're wishing that he would still love you. He doesn't love you... that's the first thing that you need to get into your head.

Graylin Cross DOES not love you...

He's willing to give himself to the red head... He's willing to give himself to Sadè and his daughter... He's willing to give himself to the little bitch that you two shared for a while but he will never give himself back to you. Now the question is...

What are you going to do about it? Continue to just accept it, or would you like to face this shit head on? There's a round trip ticket waiting for you. Go see LynMarie, confront her and make certain that she knows that he belongs to you. You leave in three days... the choice is yours...

What's it to be, Elise?

"I'm so done feeling weak," Elise felt her back straightening. "I won't let you make me feel weak any longer, Graylin. You will either love me... or you'll not love anyone... EVER."

Chapter 14: Mommy's Asleep, Kennadey

"Mr. Cross?" Graylin had become accustomed to almost hating the sound of that voice, but he turned around to face Detective Marcum. "We need to talk, Mr. Cross."

"I honestly don't have the time, Detective," he'd been standing outside trying to get a breath of fresh hair. "My daughter is in there with our family and I have to find a way to explain to her that…"

The words stopped. Graylin looked up as if hoping for some kind of answers, but all he could see were clouds. The sun was out, and it was a hot southern day. It should have been a day with him spending time with his little girl at the park or maybe even the beach, but instead he was at the hospital.

"I can't begin to say how sorry that we are Mr. Cross," Marcum reached out to touch the younger man's arm but stopped. "But, we need to do this while things are still fresh in your head."

"What things?"

"You seem to have a problem, Mr. Cross," Abraham spoke up. "The women in your life are being hurt and killed and this has put you right in the middle of everything."

"We're trying to get ahead of this, Graylin," Marcum tried to put on the calming dad's voice. "We need your help. Talk to us and let's get this over with."

Graylin stood there a moment staring at the man unsure what he wanted to say. His mind was stuck on his little girl sitting up there with his mom and dad waiting for him to come back. His thoughts were on his ex-wife and the fact that she was currently in surgery, and it wasn't looking good. He'd never say that he wanted to see Sadè dead, she was a good mom to Kenni, and even though they couldn't get along as a couple; they were good parents together.

"What happened, Son," Marcum's voice was calming. He watched as Graylin turned from him shaking his head and began pacing there in front of them. He'd only gotten a partial report when he'd gotten to the Jefferies home, and it centered around the mother being brutally attacked inside of her home. Somehow, she'd been able to call her ex-husband, who undoubtedly had their kid for the weekend, and he contacted the police.

"Talk to us, Mr. Cross," Det. Abraham had stepped into his path. "Please, tell us what you remember so that we can try to figure all of this out."

"You're homicide detectives… right?"

"Yes, Sir," she answered.

"Then why are you here? She's not…" Graylin looked from one cop to the next. "She's not dead … so what the fuck are you doing here?"

"Graylin," Marcum stepped up in front of Abraham, "the women you've been with… we have a file on all of them. You seen those folders that first time we interviewed you. From the moment that Ms. Mannsen led us to believe that you were the one who beat her, we've been investigating the people that you know. Ms. Jefferies is of course on our list and the moment her name came across the wire I knew we had to get to the crime scene."

The words "crime scene" stuck in his head. Flashes of the house and the amount of blood he'd seen before the cops arrived. The fact that he had to make certain Kenni didn't see her mom laying on the bedroom floor barely breathing. His feet were stomping into the asphalt of the parking lot as he trumped around in a circle wishing they would just leave him to deal with all of this.

"Det. Marcum," he was choking back the tears, "I need some time. Sadè is in surgery and our families are probably wondering where I'm at. My daughter is up there right now, and I need to be with her. I'll come in first thing in the morning. Please? Please, just give me tonight to make certain she's going to be okay."

"Mr. Cross," Abraham was stopped by Marcum grabbing her by the arm.

"First thing, Graylin," he'd become comfortable calling him by his first name. "We'll see you then. I hope that she pulls through the surgery and I've already put people on going through the house; the only thing is, it may be taped up for a while until we're done with our investigation."

"Don't worry about that," Graylin had turned to walk off, "I'll put her up in my house once she's released from here."

Walking back into the hospital was like walking into a morgue. There was nothing but silence. It was the quietest it had been in the hours since he'd arrived, and there was no explaining it. Every hall that he walked down was devoid of life and noise. All Graylin could hear were his own thoughts rattling through his head.

"Damn," he grumbled as he turned down the final hall staring down towards the waiting room. He could see his father pacing along the back wall and he could hear the chattering of people talking. He wanted to turn tail and walk back out because the breath of fresh air he'd gone to take was ruined by the cops. Glancing down at his watch he shook his head; it was close to midnight, and there was still no word from the doctors about the surgery.

Taking a deep breath, he walked the few paces towards the waiting area. His daughter was still awake and sitting up on his mom's lap. She jumped down calling out for him as she ran across the room and into his open arms.

"Where were you, Daddy?" She asked after kissing his cheek. "I missed you when I woke up from my nap."

"I just stepped out for a little air, Munchkin," he returned her kiss as he walked into the room hoping everyone would remain sitting. He really just needed some time because right now… nothing was making any sense. First, Elise is attacked, and he's hauled into the police station for questioning. Next, he finds out that the businesswoman killed in Denver a few months ago was actually Trinity, and now he had to deal with that being on his conscious. Now, Sadè is attack and in surgery because she was bleeding to death. How many more women he knew; that he'd slept with, were going to be hurt or killed.

Just as he sat down the doors from the surgery area opened and a slender man dressed in surgeon's scrubs walked out. The first thing that Graylin noticed was that the man looked awfully clean to have been doing any kind of operation. Even his head looked unbothered by a man who would have been standing over a body for the last four and half hours. Graylin stood.

"Jefferies family?" he nodded towards Graylin. "I'm Doctor Mallard. We were able to stop the internal bleeding, but she's very weak. Her body has gone through a lot and doing that surgery didn't make things any better. We have her resting right now in the recovery room and as soon as we can we'll be moving her to a room on the floor."

"How is she doing?" Graylin asked over the prayers and the thanks from behind him by his family and hers. "Will she be okay?"

"Right now, Sir, all we can do is wait."

"How long?"

"That's completely up to her at this point." His words were blunt but said with a softened tone as not to upset anyone. Mallard studied the eyes of the man in front of him and he wanted to give him something more to hang on to, but the truth of the matter was he gave the poor woman less than a 50% chance to recover, and if by chance she did… well, first they needed to get pass her making it through the night. He stood there answering questions as best he could, trying to give the family any semblance of hope that he could.

The room was semi lit, bit there was just enough light for her to see the measurement lines on the syringe. Aura stepped up to the bed dressed in surgical nurse scrubs and stared down at the beaten and bruised body of Sadè Jefferies. Her lips drew back into a slight smile as she stared at the now full syringe. In the dim light the pale-yellow liquid seemed almost clear.

"All you had to do was just let him see his daughter," she leaned over the prone body of the barely breathing woman. "He's mine. Do you fucking hear me, Sadè, Graylin is mine, and I'll do anything to make certain of that?

"You should have kept your fucking legs closed."

Glancing around once more, Aura slipped the needle into the port of the IV tubing and slowly pushed. "This will take a moment to do its magic," she whispered, "but you'll be one less piece in this fucked up puzzle for me to have to deal with."

She watched as the syringe emptied. The liquid mixed quickly with the clear fluids making it impossible to see. "We'll be good parents to Kennadey… I promise you that."

Aura watched for a moment longer as the solution dripped into the head of the tube pushing the fluids through and into the prone woman's body. She could only imagine the nicotine slipping into her vein and coursing through her bloodstream searching for that first open valve of her heart. She reached up touching at her own heart as if she felt that first contraction where the heart realizes that something is deathly wrong. Taking a deep breath so quickly exited the room. Once this got started it wouldn't end well and she wanted to be back home before anyone could say that she was anywhere near the hospital.

"Good bye, Sadè," she whispered to herself as she disappeared into the night.

"Doctor Mallard, to recovery room 1… stat." The monotone voice echoed from the speakers in the ceiling causing everyone to shut up at once. "Doctor Mallard, recovery room… Stat."

"Excuse me, folks," Mallard had turned to leave and was abruptly stopped by a hand pulling at his arm.

"What's going on, Doctor?" Graylin wanted to push his way by the man. "What's… is that Sadè 's room? Is something wrong or going on with her?"

"I don't know, Mr. Cross," Mallard placed a hand on the man's hand in an attempt to calm him. "I'll let you know something the moment I know something. I have to go… I'll be back, I promise."

■■■

Sadè draped her arms around Graylin' neck and leaned in to kiss his cheek. She had to giggle as he turned his head and their lips met in a soft peck. One peck became another, and another turned into a slightly passionate kiss that introduced a little tongue. His hands were at her waist pulling her against his body, but she only allowed her chest to press into his.

"Slow it down there, Mister," she pulled her lips from his and looked into his eyes. "Don't think that because you got you some the last time you were here, that you'll be getting you every time."

"Now would I think something like that?" He teased pulling her to his lips once more.

"Oh, you'll think that and a whole lot more, Graylin." Sadè pushed up from his body to stand up on the top step once more. "You need to call your daughter down, Buster, and get going."

"Damn, just kicking a brotha out just like that?"

"Yea," she winked before opening the front door, "just like that."

"That's cold, Allie," Graylin was laughing as he stepped up to the door looking in. "Ain't no naked dude in here... right?"

"Boy, stop." She slapped his shoulder. "Kennadey, your daddy's here."

His pride and joy squealed all the way to the door from upstairs. They could hear her jumping down the stairs and running through the living room and kitchen until she ran into his open arms. They hugged, and he spun them around while Sadè watched laughing.

"How's Daddy's munchkin today?"

"I am good, Daddy," her little cackling of laughter as he tickled her side. "Can we go see the monkeys at the zoo?"

"Now why would I need to go see monkeys when I got my own little monkey right here?"

Her laugh quickly became another round of squeals as both of her parents took turns tickling her. Graylin could honestly say that he missed moments like this with his family. The laughs and the playing around. He missed all of this in his life, but he didn't miss the arguing. He didn't miss the nights of waking up with her standing over him looking like she wanted to kill him. He didn't miss the accusations.

Damn, the two women he'd made his wives had a lot of similar shit about them.

"Time to go, Munchkin," he kissed her forehead. "Tell mom bye."

"You behave, Munchkin, and don't be too hard on your dad. Love you."

"Love you too, Mommy," Kennadey leaned over to kiss her mom.

"And you, Mr. Cross," she tips toed up to kiss his cheek, "thank you. Call me if you need anything."

"We'll be good," he was smiling at her. "You enjoy your time off.

Graylin loved his time with his baby girl. She was the absolute joy of his life. She was that one bright spot when shit got dark. Her laughter alone filled him to bursting, and there was nothing he wouldn't do to make her happy. She was just six, but the kid knew she had her old man wrapped around her little hand.

Sitting on the floor of the living room and eating pizza, Graylin watched her. She looked so much like Sadè. She had her mom's big brown eyes and lips. She managed to get his nose and cheeks, but her little face was still pudgy keeping her cheeks pinchable. He wondered often about how tall she would be and judging from her legs she'd be short like his grandmother.

The day had been good up to this point. He'd taken Kennadey to the zoo because she loved to see the chimpanzees. He never got tired of her excited little face the moment they walked up to the monkey pen. He stood at her side watching her and one chimp touch the glass mimicking each other trying not to laugh too loud. His phone was now full of pictures that he'd show to Sadè when he took Kenni home. The zoo had become their special place.

They'd decided on pizza and movies to end the night; for him, he'd gone with the meat lovers and for her it was pepperoni. The movie tonight was *Monster's Inc.* which happened to be her favorite movie; he always thought she had a kiddie crush on the big blue monster, Sully. They'd tossed one of his comforters on the floor and were camped out with the pizza box and their drinks enjoying the movie when his phone rang with the song he'd placed on it to let him know it was Sadè.

"Wonder what mommy wants?" he said to Kenni as he got up to get his phone from the coffee table. "Hello? Hey, Allie… you there?"

Graylin pulled the phone from his ear to make certain the phone was still there. "Sadè? Sadè, are you there?"

He could hear something, but it was faint. It was like she was breathing into the phone, but something didn't sound right. He called her name a few more times hoping that maybe she'd dialed him while she was in bed asleep… but, something still didn't sound right. He glanced over at Kennadey, she was all into her movie and for the time being that was good.

"Dammit, Sadè, answer me. What's going on? Are you, all right?"

"Graylin," her voice was barely audible. "Graylin?"

"Hey, there you are. Talk to me, Babe, what's wrong?"

Her voice faded in and out. He kept asking her what was wrong and getting no answers. His worry was growing, and he was already moving around the house to get him and Kennadey ready to go check on Sadè. Something was definitely wrong. He wanted to keep her on the phone, but he needed to call someone to get there to her.

"Graylin?"

"I'm here, Allie," he answered. "Tell me what's wrong? What's happened."

"Help me…"

"I'm coming." He turned to Kennadey, "We have to go see mommy, Munchkin, grab your shoes and head to the door."

Graylin hit the "add a call" feature on his phone and dialed 911. As the phone rang he merged the two calls so that he could hear Sadè on the other end. His patience was running thin quickly as he picked up Kenni and they were out the door just as the operator came on the line.

"911 emergency how may I help you?"

"I need someone to get to my ex-wife's home," he was trying not to yell into the phone. "I think there's something wrong."

"Wrong how, Sir?" Graylin quickly explained the call that he was on as he buckled Kenni into her booster seat.

"Please send the EMS to 9132 East Martin Luther King. I'm already on my way and I'll meet them there." Just as he said that they both could hear Sadè on the other end of the phone begging for help.

"I have emergency services and the police in route as we speak, Sir."

"Thank you… I'll be there in less than five minutes."

Graylin felt a hand on his shoulder and he looked up into his father's eyes. "I should have gotten there sooner," he shook his head. "I should have been there for her."

"You got there as fast as you could, Son," his father sat down beside him staring at his son who was staring at the door the doctor had disappeared behind. "You did everything that you could, Graylin."

"What if she…" his eyes were filling with tears as he turned to glance at his daughter playing gleefully with his mother. "What will I tell Kenni, Dad? How do I tell her that her mom is gone?"

"Don't think that way," his father wrapped an arm around his shoulder. "Sadè will be okay, Son, you just have to keep strong and have faith."

"I'm trying, Dad," he tried to be sure of his own words. "I'm trying."

∎∎∎∎

"What happened next, Graylin?" Marcum was sitting there taking notes.

"Dr. Mallard came out minutes later," Graylin was leaning over the desk with his head in his hands. "The bearer of bad news as it were. He kept apologizing and telling us that he didn't think that her heart was that weak. She'd lost a lot of blood, but they had her stabilized. He said that they knew she had a hard fight ahead of her, but her heartbeat had been strong. He didn't understand why her heart stopped; he couldn't tell us why she suddenly had a heart attack."

Marcum sat back in his chair and looked over at Abraham who was standing like a statue at his side. Once again, the words mysterious heart attack bounced around inside of his head; *that makes for three cases now, and two of which are directly connected to Graylin Cross.*

"Let's go back to when you got to the house," Marcum was studying his face.

"We've been over that twice now," Graylin was beyond aggravated.

"I want to make certain that we've covered everything. Please, once more from the beginning."

"After I got the call, I gathered up Kennadey and we rushed to the house. The front door was locked, but Sadè gave me a key so that I'd be able to get into the house if I needed to come by and get my baby something… so I let myself in. From the front door to the living room and into the kitchen it looked like a tornado had gone through the house. I sent Kennadey upstairs to her room because something didn't feel right at all."

"Where did you find Ms. Jefferies?"

"She was on the floor in the dining room area," Graylin was

rubbing his head, "and the sliding glass door was open. Not cracked... it was open."

"Did it look jimmied or pried open?"

"Did you touch anything?" Abraham interjected.

"No," Graylin cut his eyes her as if he'd been offended. "No, I didn't touch a damn thing. I know better. I was more concerned about Sadè than the goddamn door. The moment I saw her I dropped to the floor beside her and began checking her. She... she was bleeding everywhere.

"There was so much... blood. She was trying to speak, but she was choking on the blood bubbling from her lips. I couldn't do anything but pull her up into my arms and wait for the fucking EMS to get there."

"You said that she was trying to talk," Marcum cut his eyes at his partner, but she brushed him off, "were you able to understand what she was saying?"

Graylin was stressed. His little girl's mom was lying in the county morgue dead after having survived her surgery. Why? What the fuck happened after they got her into the recovery room? That doctor said that she was stable, in critical condition, but she was stable. But now she's dead. He paced the office not bothering to look at the two cops, but he could feel their eyes on him. Had she said something? His mind was blank for a moment as he tried to recall everything that had happened. She kept mumbling. She kept trying to get him to listen, but he was more concerned with the gaping hole in her chest.

Her voice was weak. Her body felt so cold and she was trembling. He could feel her fingers, sticky with her blood on his face trying to pull his ear to her mouth. The blood was drool from between her lips, but they were moving.

"Not... blue," he mumbled to himself trying to recall her words. "Not blue... they were green."

"Excuse me?" Abraham stepped up to the edge of the desk. "What are you talking about, Mr. Cross?"

"She was telling me, not blue, they were green."

"Do you have any idea what she was talking about?" Marcum asked.

"No," Graylin could picture her beautiful face covered in her blood, and the EMS had finally arrived. The house was suddenly full of noise and activity as the emergency people and the police were now crowding in around him. The cops were trying to pull him from his ex-wife as the EMS men were checking her vitals and quickly trying to get her ready to be moved. He stood there watching. His body felt stuck in place and he didn't hear a word that the cops were saying. Nothing at this point was making any sense to him, and all he could do was watch as everything happened in slow motion.

"No, I have no clue what she meant." He turned to face the two detectives. "I don't understand any of this, and I don't know why this shit is happening to me."

"Not trying to be rude, Graylin," he shook his head, "but that's three women that you've been involved with being either attacked or dying of mysterious causes. First, we have Trinity Wheeling and her heart attack right in front of her business, one of your ex-wives being beaten and now the other one dying... of a heart attack. What do you make of all of this?"

"If I had any answers to that," Graylin looked up angrily, "that would make me the detective and not either of you... now wouldn't it. Look, I came in here like I promised and now I feel like you're back to accusing me for shit I had nothing to do with."

"Is that what's happening, Det. Marcum? Am I a suspect again?"

"That's to be determined," Abraham interjected before Marcum could answer.

"What the fuck does that mean... to be determined?" Graylin pushed back from the desk and jumped up. "I was home with my goddamn daughter and you're telling me I may be a fucking suspect in her mother's death. Do you know what I had to tell a fucking five-year-old when she asked me where's her mom?

"Well do you, Detectives?" he stared at the two them as they both followed his pacing around the office. "I had to tell her... Shhhh, it's going to all be ok, mommy's asleep, Kennadey... mommy's asleep."

Chapter 15: One More to Go

Aura felt hidden amongst the throng of people moving around in the airport. She'd just seen Graylin off to see his publisher. Now she was watching as Elise picked up her ticket to go see LynMarie. The flight to Texas would only be a couple of hours, and she had every intention of just sitting back and watching.

There was a moment when she just wanted to walk to the other woman and just slap her. She was unsure why though. Aura sat with a wide brimmed hat pulled low over her face, so Elise wouldn't recognize her. She was such a pitiful sight. She'd lost quite a bit of weight in the last few weeks, and her face had healed nicely from the self-inflicted bruises.

"Such a pitiful creature," Aura murmured pretending to read the magazine she held. "Still, though, beating the shit out of yourself was quite a sight to watch."

She'd been standing at the sliding glass door at the back of Elise's house the night she'd decided to beat the shit out of herself against a wall in the living room. Impressed that this woman was willing to do to herself what she had every intention of doing to her that very night had put a smile on her face. Her only wish is that she could have been there when the police had pulled Graylin from his home. She chuckled to herself before looking around to see if there was anyone watching.

Elise had finally picked up her ticket and was making her way towards the departure gate. Aura sat waiting patiently before going to check herself. The walk to the gate was quick and she made certain to keep away from Elise. She kept a close eye on the woman as they both waited for the plane to finally dock and release its current passengers.

The trip was not a bad one. Aura sat in coach and had been one of the first to board the plane. This gave her time to get settled into her seat and again just watch. Elise was a few rows ahead of her and was walking around as if her head were in the clouds. Aura smiled. She sat in her seat wondering just what could be going through Elise's head. Maybe she was trying to figure out just what she would say to LynMarie. Maybe she was wondering why in the hell she would listen to a mysterious person and even get on this plane. Whatever it was, Elise looked pretty spooked by her decision to take a trip to Texas, her own home state.

"This is completely beautiful," Aura whispered to herself.

Settling back into her seat, Aura got comfortable for the flight. Her row neighbor was particularly chatty and through a force of nature she kept up the lighthearted conversation until the plane began to taxi down the runway.

"I think I'm going to shut my eyes for a bit," she informed the older lady sitting at the window.

"I'll wake you when we're making our approach," the lady responded with a friendly smile.

"Thank you." Aura took another look up the aisle to see that Elise had pulled out her laptop and she smiled. She pulled out her phone and quickly sent her a text message.

I see that you've decided to take me up on your little trip. You have a safe flight and do not worry yourself with what you're going to say to the little bitch... everything will come out just as it should when you see her. Just remember...

This is for Graylin. This is for what's yours.

Elise read the email once more before laying her head back against the seat. Her mind was all over the place. Her stomach was bouncing around; one because she hated flying and two because facing LynMarie was something she hadn't thought of doing for years. Her memories of the younger woman had been quite fond for the longest time and then she'd remember the moment she was sure that Graylin was falling for their shared "toy". Her hatred for the girl was subtle at first, and then she found out that he was still talking to her even after she'd begged him to stop.

"Are you fucking kidding me, Elise," it was the first time in quite a while that she'd seen him so mad. "You put spyware on my goddamn computer and thought I wouldn't figure it out? Are you fucking serious?"

"I just thought…"

"No, you didn't think at all," he was storming around the house like a maniac. "You didn't think at all."

"Why the hell are you so mad, Graylin?" she asked him. "What, were you afraid that I'd find out that you're still talking to that little slut?"

"I don't give a damn what you find out, Elise," he was up in her face not quite screaming or yelling. "I don't hide shit because I don't have shit to fucking hide. You could have asked me, and I would have told you, but no, you thought it was something smart to put this shit on the computer."

"I'm sorry," she whined feeling quite small at this point.

"I've always told you, if I was cheating on you I wouldn't be stupid enough to get caught. I don't do shit that I feel I have to hide from you or anyone else for that goddamn matter. And yet... I constantly have to deal with this kind of bullshit."

"What about the email, Graylin? What about all of that shit in the email? Have you really been seeing her since I asked you not to?"

"I wondered just how long before you read that," he'd walked off and fixed him a drink and was swallowing deeply. "I knew you was reading shit on my laptop. I could tell when your ass had been on there and so I wanted to see exactly what you were up to. I made up that email account just to catch your ass, and I had that email sent to me just to see when you would go into it. And your ass didn't disappoint."

"What?" she stood staring at him horrified.

"Yea, that's right, Elise... it was a fucking plant. Thank you for showing me just what the hell I'm dealing with."

She watched as the man she loved more than anything in this world stormed from the house grabbing his jacket and keys. She stood at the window crying as he jumped into his car and with a loud screeching peal of rubber he drove out of their neighborhood.

Elise wiped a tear from her eye as she closed her laptop. She'd messed up so much with Graylin and the only thing she ever wanted was for him to realize that she loved him. She wanted him to know that she would do anything to prove that she loved him. Sitting on the plane she now wondered if this was the wrong move. Something inside of her was telling her that she was making the same mistakes that she'd been making over the course of their relationship.

But it was too late...

The plane taking off made her stomach unsettled, but she held her breath. Slowly it passed, and she settled back into her seat closing her eyes. the trip wouldn't take but a couple of hours and she could at least thing on what she would do during that time. A part of her hoped that she would just sit at the airport waiting for her return flight, but she knew once she got to Houston she would leave the airport and she would make her way to the address she'd been given by her mysterious benefactor.

"What's in this for you?" she asked. "Why are you doing this for me?"

The plane landed.

"Oh damn, Elise? What are you doing here?" LynMarie's mouth dropped open as she stood in her doorway staring at a woman she thought she'd never have to see again. The past flashed before her and images of them three of them filled her head. She refused to step aside as Elise tried to step forward and into her home. "Why are you here?"

"Are you alone, LynMarie?"

"No," she lied thankful that her husband wasn't home. "Why are you here?"

LynMarie stepped out of her house and faced Elise. The bad blood between them had never been on her part, but over the last couple of years she'd grown to hate this woman. Elise was the reason that Graylin had stopped talking to her. In his mind he was trying to save her. He'd explained it a million times, but none of them ever settled with her. She'd wanted to be with him, and at one point with the both of them.

She stood in front of Elise with her arms folded over her chest. Her eyes were quickly taking in the neighborhood to see if there was anyone out, and thankful that the streets looked clear; well almost clear, she had to keep from waving at Mrs. Landry because the nosy old lady would have taken that a gesture to come over. She stepped away towards the front of the garage not waiting to see if Elise followed.

"I'll ask once more," she said turning to face the woman, "why the hell are you here, Elise?"

"I know that you've seen him." Her statement was blunt and to the point. "Why?"

"Why is that any of your business?" LynMarie refused to back down. "What Graylin does now that he isn't with your crazy ass is his own business."

"You need to understand one thing, Girl," Elise was up in LynMarie's face before she could step back, "Graylin is still my goddamn husband. There's been no divorce and there won't be one if I have anything to do with it."

"See, this is why he's left you, Elise," LynMarie smiled. "You have no clue who he is. You don't think about him and only about yourself. You need to grow the fuck up and get the fuck on. Leave that man alone and go on with your life."

"Graylin is my life," Elise tempered her voice to keep from screaming. "You need to just leave him alone."

"And what if he doesn't want to leave me alone, Elise," her smile spoke volumes. "What if Graylin wants more of what he got the last time we were together? What if he wants to skip dinner all together and just take me back to his hotel and fuck the living hell out of me over and over and ov…"

The slap to her face stopped her words but didn't remove the smile. LynMarie could feel the tears burning her eyes. Her cheek was on fire as she reached up rubbing it.

"Some things just never change, do they, Elise." She licked her lip to make certain there was no blood. "Does he know about our last meeting? Did you tell your 'husband' about how you came to my apartment and threatened to kill me if I even called him again?"

Elise backed away turning her back to LynMarie. Once again, the thoughts of why she was really here stomped through her head like a herd of elephants. Graylin would never forgive her for even being here, and yet all she wanted to do was turn around and slap her face once more.

"You're really trying my patience, LynMarie," she said not bothering to turn around. "I want you to leave my Husband alone. Don't answer anymore of his calls. When he comes to this wretched city, don't even think about seeing him. Nothing. Absolutely nothing from you ever again, LynMarie, because if I find out I'll be back here, and I'll beat you to within an inch of your life with your husband sitting there watching."

"I'm not afraid you," LynMarie had walked up on her and spun her around. Before Elise could defend herself, the hand connected with her face harder than anything had ever done. She'd never worried about a man ever slapping her, but this girl... "You cannot tell me what to do anymore, Elise. Don't you ever presume to think that I'm still that same naïve girl you met all of those years ago."

The force of the hit was enough to make her stumble a bit. Her eyes were shut tight trying to close out the sparks of light bursting. One hand went to her mouth to keep her from crying out, and the other flopped around trying to keep her from falling. The world felt all upside down, and as it slowly settled she opened her eyes to stare at the younger woman standing in front of her. She noticed immediately that LynMarie had her fists balled and the look in her eyes implied that she was ready to hurt someone.

"You need to leave my home, Elise," LynMarie's teeth were grinding together as she spoke. "You need to leave, and your best bet is to never come back."

Elise walked away feeling a lot like scolded dog. She'd come to Houston to teach this little tease a lesson, but she was the one put in place. She felt stupid. Her face hurt from the slap and she was on the verge of tears. She felt weak. She had once been the first girl to Graylin and LynMarie was under her, but right now, she felt lower than she'd ever thought of this girl.

She snatched open her door and dropped in the seat. LynMarie was watching her and her fists were still clenched tightly. Her brow was furrowed, but she remained in her yard... watching. As she started her car, the new phone she'd had to purchase chimed with a new text message.

You need to leave now, Elise. Your time here in Houston is over and you proved that you can take a slap quite well. Your flight leaves in about 2 hours... I'll be seeing you very soon. I think it's time to meet...
Don't You?

The smile that crowned Aura's face was priceless. She'd had a car rental waiting for her the moment they touched ground and not waiting for Elise to catch a cab she drove out to the address she'd been given. Parking, she waited for the upcoming fireworks, and then it would be her turn. If this all worked out the way she'd pictured it in her head, there were a few people in the neighborhood who'd seen this very argument and could readily describe Elise to the police. The set up was finally coming together, and hopefully the police back home were finally getting the evidence against Elise concerning the death of her first husband.

She'd put a lot of time and money into everything that has happened up to this point. She'd followed Elise since the first time she found out about the Number One Graylin Cross fan club website the woman had put up. She fed into the woman's obsession with Graylin. She'd even gotten to know her by becoming one of her online friends and posting pictures that she knew Elise could never get her hands on. This part of the set up was easy, and the reason made as much sense today as it did.

Elise should have stayed away from him...

"This is too beautiful," she was grinning as she watched Elise slap the taste from LynMarie's little pouty mouth.

How she hated all of these women, and all for the same reason. Graylin Cross. He was supposed to fall in love with her, and yet he was always paying these other bitches too much goddamn attention. Who's been there for him more than any of these women starting with that first ex-wife, Sadè? She'd been there for him helping him to build the kind of fan base that most unknown authors will never know. She got his name and his books into the some of the most sought-after book clubs, and before he even knew what happened... Graylin Cross was a household name.

She'd actually found out about him when she was first approached by Mishelle Rivers to be his personal assistant. Mishelle had given her a couple of his first books to read to get an idea of the material she would be working with, and it was an instant love affair with his words. The first time they met it took everything in her not to just attack him right there, but she kept calm and showed her most professional place. Inside she was boiling over. After that meeting she rushed home and just about raped her then, live-in boyfriend before asking him to leave.

Aura sat in her car watching as the little bit of drama across the street began to unfold. It wouldn't get too bad. Elise would never do anything but talk shit. LynMarie she wasn't sure about, but after watching her reaction after being slapped… she would have to be careful when she confronted her.

"Slap her ass back," she whispered. She watched as LynMarie walked up on Elise while her back was turned. The entire scene was something beautiful. LynMarie had grabbed Elise and spun her around and before Elise could react she was slapped so hard that Aura thought she heard it.

"Damn," Aura was almost giddy. She could see Elise trying not to cry. LynMarie was now stalking her and backing her up the drive way towards the road. From across the street she could see a spark that she hadn't expected in LynMarie, and it fascinated her for a moment.

She knew of the little threesome tryst between Graylin and these two women. She'd watched their little escapades on a number of occasions. She had every reason to hate LynMarie, but she didn't. At this point, LynMarie was merely a means to an end; that end being watching Elise fall off into her own personal hell. Aura watched as Elise was told to leave and rather cowardly… she walked away. LynMarie had stood her ground and won their little pissing match, and Aura was impressed.

Pulling out her phone, smiling from her front row seat, Aura quickly typed out a message and sent the text to Elise. The ruse had to be continued for just a little longer, but the time for all of this was coming to an end. She'd grown tired of the game. She'd been at this for longer than she cared to think about, and now she wanted it over. She was tired of toying with Elise's life, and she was tired of the bodies. There'd been so much death she'd have to wash from her hands. There was so much blood. She was sick of it all, and just longed for a peaceful life with the man of her dreams. She longed to be…

Mrs. Graylin Cross.

You need to leave now, Elise. Your time here in Houston is over

and you proved that you can take a slap quite well. Your flight leaves in about 2 hours… I'll be seeing you very soon. I think it's time to meet…
Don't You?

But for now, the blood would remain. It would be a little thicker on her hands after what she intended to do once Elise was gone. She glanced over after sending the message watching as Elise drove off, and her eyes fell on her next intended victim.

It was early still, and she'd wait for it to become dark before entering the house. It was her intentions to catch her off balance, and just as she had with Trinity Grey, she'd plunge the needle of her syringe into that delicate neck. She'd press her thumb down watching the liquid in the clear tubing slowly push into her young body. Then she would leave her to die.

"It's all too beautiful," she smiled as she got comfortable. It would be night soon enough.

Chapter 16: "Everything We Thought is Wrong."

"Something is just not right," Marcum declared as he stomped in a circle in front of Capt. Rowlings desk. "Everything just seems to be lining up and pointing right at Elise Mannsen, but…"

"But, what?" Rowlings was seated looking through the stacks of papers settled on her desktop.

"But, it's not adding up, Enessa," he'd looked to make certain that they were alone. "Look at everything there. I've gone through it a million times and even though the circumstantial evidence all points neatly towards this woman… my gut tells me that something is not right."

Enessa had been keeping up to date on this case since the night they'd almost wrongfully arrested Graylin Cross. She'd always known Marcum to be a very meticulous detective. He was never one to bulldog one suspect without a doubt that was his man. If she knew anything about the man, she knew that he was looking at this from more angles and necessary.

"What are you thinking, Erick?" She was trusting his judgment.

"I think that I need to back to the beginning," he turned to look at her. "I need to go to Texas and talk to the police there that investigated her first husband's death. I think my answers lie there."

"I'll call downstairs and get the voucher that you'll need for the ticket," Rowlings stood and walked from behind her desk. "I'm going in on this with you, Erick, but if you don't find whatever it is you think you're missing… we arrest Elise Mannsen."

"Agreed," he stood there staring at his former partner. "You're a damn good captain, Nessa, thank you for trusting me again."

"You've never let me down," she smiled patting his shoulder. "You're a good detective and I can tell when you're on to something that makes sense. I'm with you on this, everything is just all too neat. All of it pointing right at this one woman and yet, other than stalking her husband, I just don't see her for the deaths."

"So, you think she's stalking Cross too?"

"With all of the stuff that man's been telling us, not to mention the restraining order that he has in place," Rowlings shrugged her shoulders, "it's hard not to believe she's stalking him."

"Very true, but that's something he'll have to deal with on a later note." Marcum almost laughed.

"You get going," Rowlings was back behind her desk picking up the phone. "I'll get my end done, but you need to get there get your information and get back here so we can wrap this up before anyone else is hurt or killed."

"Yes, Ma'am."

"Be careful out there, Erick," she warned. "I want you back here safe and sound. Do you understand me?"

"I understand completely, Nessa," he grinned and before opening the door quickly added. "And I love you too."

■■■

Graylin was no stranger to death or funerals. As a writer, he wrote about death and murder on a daily basis. He'd studied it. He'd made himself a self-made expert on a number of ways death could occur. He was a fan of the macabre. Hell, unknown to most, Halloween was his absolute favorite holidays of the year. He was no stranger to death at all, but he was a stranger to his daughter hurting.

He and Kennadey sat in the front of the church that he and Sadè had been married in. They were surrounded on both sides by his family and Sadè's family. It was possibly the worse day he could imagine as his little girl sat huddled into his side trying not to stare at the coffin that was front and center. He couldn't blame her. He was trying hard to imagine that the damn thing wasn't sitting there. He was trying to pretend that Sadè was sitting beside him on one side and their baby on the other, but he failed.

His sunglasses were dark enough that they hid his eyes. His hand was gently patting Kenni's back as she softly sobbed into his suit jacket. He'd dressed her in a beautiful little pink dress so that she wouldn't look like everyone else in the church dressed in all black and white. He'd opted for one of his gray pin stripped suits that he'd had tailored a few months ago for a television interview that had been canceled. He felt sick to his stomach right now but tried to keep calm for his daughter's sake.

The services hadn't started yet, and the number of people walking up to offer their condolences was already disturbing. He knew most of them. He'd grown up with quite a few of them. There were people he was sure Sadè had worked with, and of course there were those who no one knew. Outside he could only imagine the media circus that was setting up, because it had been splashed all through the news…

"Local Best-Selling Author, Graylin Cross, to attend funeral

service for his ex-wife and mother to his only child, Sadè Jefferies."

He sat there wondering who he could sue for disrupting this time with his family to be disturbed by all of that nonsense. He was using any and everything he could to take his mind from the here and now, as the reverend finally made his way to the pulpit.

"Now for the real circus," he thought. Glancing around Graylin picked out at least three people that he was sure would be falling out in the aisle screaming and hollering. He found another half dozen he was positive would dance their way to the front screaming they got the Holy Ghost.

Graylin reached down and pulled Kennadey up to hold her to him. He needed her to keep him grounded. He needed his baby to keep him from going off on all of these people. This was going to be a long day. A very, very long day.

"Please just let me make through this in one peace," he prayed as the service began.

Reverend Thompson met him at the door as he was heading for the limousine waiting for him and Kennadey. The man was younger than him, but he'd delivered a powerful sermon for Sadè 's funeral service. Graylin was actually quite amazed. He hadn't been inside of a church since he and Elise had married. He was never much for churches and was quite fortunate that his parents were the type to force it upon him or his siblings. He stopped and shook the younger man's hand and thanked him.

"I just want to personally offer my condolences to you and your daughter for your loss, Mr. Cross," Rev. Thompson held on to Graylin' hand with both of his own. "Please, do not hesitate to come to me if you're in need of anything."

"Thank you, Reverend," Graylin was unsure how to address him. "I wanted to thank you for the sermon. And, I want to apologize for all of this."

They both looked out at the throng of reporters and news cameras forming a semi-circle just past the line of cars that would be heading towards the burial site. The reverend shook his head but smiled.

"We all have our cross to bear, Mr. Cross."

"Very true," Graylin returned the smile. "We'll see you at the gravesite."

The walk down the steps towards his limo felt longer than he could have imagine. He felt like a man on death row walking the "Mile" to his final fate. He felt himself watching his feet. Each step was measured and even calculated to make certain that he didn't misstep sending him tumbling forward with Kennadey in his arms. He could hear them screaming out questions concerning his relationship with Sadè, but he ignored them all. There were a few police there, thanks to Mishelle, and they kept the vultures back from him and everyone in the car train. He finally made it to the car and stepped in greeted by his parents and Sadè's mom.

"It's like a zoo out there," he tried to joke it off. "I'm sorry about all of that."

"Get in, Son," his father reached out and took Kennadey. "This is just bound to be a long day with everything that's going on."

"Yea," Graylin stepped into the limousine and tried to get comfortable. "I'll be glad to just get home and try to... I don't know... I really don't..."

His voice trailed off as he turned as they were sliding the coffin into the back of the hearse. He'd walked out after them, but they were just putting her into the back of the large black car. His heart sunk. He and Sadè were the type of couple that would have never gotten back together. They both knew that it was better for them to be apart.

"I miss her..." he heard Kennadey tell her grandpa. "I miss my mommy."

"I do too," he whispered. "More than anyone would ever guess."

■■■■

"Good afternoon, Captain Hilliard," Marcum walked in with his hand out, "I'm Detective Erick Marcum. I think we spoke on the phone a couple of times."

"Yes, Sir," the captain stood accepting the other man's hand. "The Kaine case, correct?"

"Yes, Terrence Kaine." Marcum stood waiting to be offered a seat. Once the captain sat he followed suite in the first available chair in front of the man's desk. "I know that you've been investigating the case, but we have a case back home that bares resemblances to this case and I'm just here to see if I can dot the I's on our case."

"Resemblances in what way, Detective?"

"Your second autopsy found traces of nicotine, pure nicotine that your coroner is now convinced created Kaine's heart attack. Correct?"

"Well you've definitely done your homework," Hilliard slid a folder across the desk allowing Marcum a moment to look through it. "We had to exhume the body at the request of the family because they were not happy or content with the initial results."

"Capt. Hilliard, who found Kaine? How long had he been dead before the body was found?"

"Found… found," Hilliard was thumbing through his notes. "The mother was the one to call in the body. He was apparently staying with his folks at the time of his death and was found in the trailer that they had on their back property. From the report, Kaine and the Mrs. we're separating, and he was keeping the baby boy."

"Hm," Marcum grunted. "What makes no sense to me right now is, why would she kill him when he had the baby and she was pretty much free of him? That just seems like a bit much…. don't you think so?"

"I really don't pretend to understand why these people do the things that they do, Detective," Hilliard stated without a real care. "My job is to find them and hand them over to the state to prosecute. I don't want to know why. From what I figured, maybe there was some domestic stuff that we just never knew about, and she just got tired of him. It seems to happen all of the time."

"Yea," Marcum mumbled. "Maybe…"

Marcum was thumbing through the papers in the file reading everything that came across as being important. He stopped at the interview with Elise Mannsen. Once again that feeling in his gut that things were not adding up correctly burned. As he read the interview he noticed that her answers had her out of town.

"Damn," he murmured.

"What is it, Detective?"

"Elise Mannsen stated that she was out of town on the date of his death. Was that ever established?"

"I know my officers looked into it, but I cannot recall if there was ever anything verified on that matter." Hilliard was looking through another set of notes. "She'd stated that she was at some kind of book convention but couldn't produce any names of anyone who may have seen her there."

"How long was she there?"

"We were able to find out that there was a three-day convention scheduled for the time she'd said she was out of town." Hilliard slid another piece of paper across the desk. "There about 15 to 20 authors on the docket and a number of talks. It was a big to do at the time because a few major names had been dropped to be there."

"Is Elise still one of your primary suspects," Marcum was reading the notes on the new piece of paper.

"We don't have enough on her, and we were never able to find anyone else." Hilliard said bluntly. "When she left, we were able to keep track of her whereabouts for a while. I would say until your call it had been two or maybe three years."

Marcum spotted the name on the list of authors that he was looking for and sat back in the chair. His mind was racing. Everything he'd been coming across had been leading him in the wrong direction. It had all been forcing him to consider the one person that made the near perfect candidate. He pulled his notepad from his jacket and flipped through a few pages.

"It's all been way too neat for me," he stated. "Everything pointing to her, and yet..."

"And yet, what?"

"I don't think Elise is responsible, but I don't think I have enough to... say that definitively."

"What do you need, Det. Marcum?"

"We need to find out if she was really at this convention," he stared at the names on the list once again. "I have to make a call."

Marcum stood and walked from the office. He needed some fresh air, but more importantly, he needed some privacy when he called Cross. He wasn't surprised when his name showed up on the list. In fact, he was counting on it. Now the question is, can Cross think back three years to remembering talking to Elise?

"Come on, answer the goddamn phone, Cross," he said holding the phone to his ear.

■■■■

The last few days have been murder. With the burial of Sadè behind them, now Graylin and Kennadey had to readjust their living relationship. She loved being at his house, but never this long. A couple of days at most and then she was ready to go back home to her mommy. He could hear her sometimes late at night calling out for Sadè and he just wanted to run in there and hold her. He'd been waking up with her lying in his bed curled up under him and sucking her thumb.

They'd enjoy a little breakfast. He'd get her off to school and make it back home to work. To work. To... work. The words were lost to him, and he couldn't stand sitting at his desk staring at the blank page on his computer. He'd heard from Mishelle and she had insisted that he needed to take some time off and just deal with being with his daughter full time.

But, he needed to keep busy; that's what he'd told her, and he'd repeated to himself over and over.

Graylin stared at his screen. The pages previous had a hellava story on them, and he was so close to finishing this book. His brain wasn't in. His thoughts were everywhere except for the writing. Too much has happened in the last few months that he was completely off his game. His concentration was shot. He'd gotten into drinking like he was a teenager fresh out of high school and his parents' house. He tried to stay sober during the day, but the moment he'd put Kenni down…

"Dammit," he'd grabbed the bottle of bourbon sitting on his desk and thrown it across the room. He pushed back from the desk and grabbed the chair and it was tossed as well. Everything but the computer was swept from the top of the desk. He stomped across the room and threw every bottle of liquor on the small bar watching as they crashed against the wall and their contents streamed down the paint.

All he saw was red. He couldn't describe what he was feeling. All he saw was red, and like a bull he thundered forward. Everything felt his wrath as he stormed around the office tearing up everything he could get his hands on. First, he's pulled into the police station and questioned because Elise had had the shit beaten out of her, or had she? He was breathing heavy, standing in the middle of the mess he'd made bent over and holding onto his knees to keep from falling. He'd seen the things she was capable of, but he wasn't sure if she could beat herself senseless. Could she have someone do it for her? Or maybe, maybe she was truly attacked?

Graylin walked over the sofa that he upturned and set it upright. He sat down staring off into space. His head was a mess with a million thoughts all at one time. The beating, Trinity's death, now Sadè's death… who could have wanted all of this to take place? For the first time since all of this began, he thought about everything. The pieces were all over the place, and none of it was making sense.

Not blue… they were green.

"What am I missing?" he questioned. "What the hell were you trying to tell me, Sadè?"

Somewhere in the mess he'd made he could hear his phone ringing. Graylin jumped up following the sound of his ringtone. Finding it, he looked at the screen, but didn't recognize the number.

"This is Graylin Cross," he answered.

"Graylin, good you answered." Graylin almost didn't recognize the voice. "It's Det. Marcum."

"Yes," he acknowledges the response as he walked back to his sofa and sat down. "How can I help you, Detective?"

"I need to know how good your memory is?"

"Okay," Graylin was confused.

"You were at a convention in Texas about three maybe four years ago."

"Yeah," Graylin was already searching through his memories about that convention. It had been in Dallas, and he'd been surprised when Aura had gotten him not only a spot at the convention. He was also a part of a celebrity of authors panel that got to be questioned by the crowd. "One of the major highlights of my career, Detective. Why do you ask?"

"Do you recall the discussion we had about Elise and the husband she never told you about?"

"You're walking be around in circles, Det. Marcus," he was getting irritated. "I remember the discussion and I remember the convention, now tell me what's this about?"

"During the time you were at that convention, Elise's husband Terrence Kaine was killed… she may have been at that convention. Do you remember seeing her? Did Elise come to see you during that time?"

Finally, for months now, Graylin had been trying to figure out why the obsession? Why did it feel like he'd met her before that day in the book store? He almost dropped the phone as he sat there letting his eyes search the crowd of that convention.

"She was there," his voice was barely audible. "All this time, I've been trying think of where I'd seen her, and it was right there. Her blue eyes… her goddamn blue eyes!"

He remembered her clearly. She was incredibly beautiful. He could see her slowly moving through the crowd, first she was pretending to ignore him, but then her path became quite clear. She was making her way to see him. The dress she'd worn was black, tight and stopped just above her knees. The neckline was deep, and he had to draw his eyes away from her cleavage to look up into her eyes. He was still sitting so he was looking up into those beautiful, blue eyes.

"Hello, Mr. Cross," her voice filled his head and her smile teased his eyes. He reached out for her book to sign, and she gently took his hand into hers and shook. Her eyes were dazzling, the bluest eyes he'd ever seen. They were like looking into the ocean and the heavens at one time and getting completely lost. He was enraptured. He was entranced, and she knew it.

"Dammit," Graylin grunted.

"Graylin, I'm in Texas right now," Marcum's voice had reached him in deep thoughts, "but I'll be on a plane in a few hours. I need to see you immediately. Everything that we thought about this case… is wrong. It's not your ex-wife killing the women in your life."

Graylin agreed to meet with Marcum, but his mind was still going through everything. The pieces of the puzzle. Those things that kept a writer writing was bringing all the pieces together at the end to compete the picture. Now it was time for him to unravel the pieces. He needed to figure out what he was missing. What Marcum had said made a lot of sense…

Everything that we thought about this case is wrong.

"Exactly," he said aloud. "But the question is… who benefits from Elise going to prison and for Trinity and Sadè being… dead?"

Graylin sat up on the edge of the sofa and grabbed the phone he'd dropped beside him and he dialed a number. He sat waiting for an answer.

"Come on, LynMarie," he murmured as the phone continued to ring. "Pick up the goddamn phone… SHIT."

Chapter 17: Unwinding the Mystery

Aura sat on the bed watching Graylin walk around the bedroom. She'd let herself in, which was the norm, a few hours ago to find him up and about already. She was rather impressed at how well he'd become accustomed to being a full-time father. Kennadey was a beautiful little girl, and Aura fell in love with her from the moment she'd met her. Graylin was absolutely great with her, and Aura couldn't wait to see how he'd be with their…

"Damn," he slammed his fist against the wall. "This shit is just fucking crazy."

"What's wrong, Graylin?" she stood for a moment to sit back down on one of her legs. "What's crazy?"

Graylin turned. He stared at the woman for a moment as if trying to figure out why she was here. His mornings were better when it was just him after he'd taken Kennadey to school. It gave him a moment to try to collect himself after a night of drinking. He took a deep breath. He'd have to pretend that she wasn't sitting on his bed dressed in just one of his shirts. She was always there to … tempt him.

Thoughts were now swimming around in his head. As he was about to mention her attire, his phone rang. It was LynMarie and he hurriedly answered the call.

"LynMarie? I've been calling you. Are you alright?"

The look on Aura's face was unreadable, but unmistakable. He pressed his back to the wall and just stood watching her as she fidgeted on the bed.

"Elise was here, Graylin," LynMarie's voice got his attention.

"What? When was Elise there?"

"Just a few days ago," LynMarie told him. "We pretty much got into each other's face right there in front of my house. My goddamn husband was fucking home when she showed up at my door."

"How the fuck did she even know where you lived?" Graylin was still watching Aura; her head was dropped, but he could tell she was all into his call.

"I don't know," LynMarie groaned out like she was in pain. "What I do know is after I slapped the shit out of her and made her ass leave… I got attacked just a couple of hours later."

"Wait a minute," Graylin felt like his head was in a whirlwind, "back up for a sec… what the fuck did Elise want?"

"She wanted to remind me that you're hers. The main thing she kept saying was that she didn't want me talking to you. She was very adamant that you were still married to her and that she still loved you."

"Damn."

"That bitch is crazy, Graylin," LynMarie sounded scared for him. "You need to get her out of your life completely. She's completely unstable, and she's bound to do anything. And I heard about the death of your first ex-wife."

Graylin hadn't hidden anything from LynMarie. She knew about Sadè and Kennadey, she'd even talked to Kenni on the phone a few times.

"Getting her out of my life is top on my list of things," he said softly. "She'll be getting served very soon, but I'm worried about you. You said that you were attacked? What happened after Elise left?"

"James and I were upstairs, and I'd come back down to get him something to drink and to check the house. I never seen who it was, Graylin, but she hit me from behind when I was checking to see why the sliding glass door was open. She was on me before I could react, and we were rolling around on the floor. I cannot be sure if it was Elise; I mean she had dark hair, but there was something about her eyes."

"Something like what?" Graylin found himself watching his words.

"They were blue, but not a clear blue," LynMarie said. "It's like she was wearing contacts. I would swear that I saw green, but she was choking me, and I was fighting to just fucking breathe."

"What else happened?" He'd heard what she'd said but thought it best not to repeat it. His mind was going a million miles a minute. His eyes hadn't left Aura, and she still wasn't looking up at him. Everything was completely off about all of this.

"She had me pinned to the floor and had pressed a needle into the side of my neck. I didn't know what she was trying to get into me, and I'm thankful that James was there. He pulled her off and she ran off. The doctor said that if she'd got anymore of the pure nicotine into my system. The way the doctor explained it, it would have been like I was having a massive heart attack. Whoever she was she tried to kill me."

"Yea," his voice was almost a whisper. "It would have. I'm sorry, LynMarie, all of this shit is my fault. I'm trying to wrap my mind around all of this, but right now I'll be completely honest… I'm fucking stomped. Hey look, if you don't wish to talk to me after this I completely understand."

"Whoever that was, Graylin, cannot scare me away from you anymore than Elise could. I'm looking forward to seeing you again... and very soon too."

"You have my word," he was smiling. "Let me know when they're releasing you from the hospital."

Aura stood and began looking around for her clothes. There would be no seducing him this morning, and it would be better to leave. She could feel his eyes on her as she bent over to pick up the shorts and the top she'd worn over. Her heart was pounding. LynMarie was still alive and now Graylin was staring at her funny. She was trying to keep her breathing easy, and yet the weirdest thing was, all of this was exciting her beyond words. Her legs trembled just a bit, and she could feel her mound getting hotter... wetter. She wondered if he could smell the fragrant aroma of her excitement.

"You seem a little..." he paused watching as she removed his shirt and tossed it to the bed, "A little... nervous."

Standing naked in front of this man truly made her feel nervous every time. She always wondered what he thought about her body? If liked what he saw? Or if he just fucked her because she gave it to him whenever he wanted? She wanted him to love her the way she loved him, but he'd been a little distant since her little outcry.

"You know I love it when you look at me, Graylin," she tried playing off the phone call conversation. "You make me nervous because all I want to do is please you."

"Please me," Graylin stared at her. There was no doubting that she was beautiful. He'd always loved a woman with longer hair because he loved pulling it, but her short pixie cut always seemed to fit her face. She was so pale but her green eyes always seemed to just pop as one of her best features, and her red lips... He took a deep breath, as he allowed his eyes to soak her in.

His hands had been all over body. He'd touched and stroked her until she'd scream out his name loud enough to scare the neighbors. Her breasts were full and filled his hands and her nipples were the most sensitive that he'd ever played with. She was always hot. He never had to worry about her being excited. And, she was always willing to try the things he'd stressed he wanted to do.

For the first time he was actually looking at the woman. His mind kept going over that day she'd screamed out that she loved him. Her body was close enough to an orgasm that he'd just accepted it as her screaming out in passion. But now, standing here staring at her, there was something different in his thought process. There was something that he just couldn't put his finger on. He held his tongue as she finished dressing.

"Please me, huh?" he repeated.

"I've always wanted to please you, Graylin," she smiled big hoping to ease the discomfort laying over the room. Her mind was screaming for her to leave. She needed time to go and regroup after hearing about LynMarie. She'd hoped that enough of the nicotine had been pushed into her before the husband found them. Now she knew it hadn't and that could fuck up everything.

"Yea," he chuckled and relaxed. "You're right, and I do appreciate you in ways you'd never believe."

"I would believe anything you told me," she chuckled as well.

"So where are you running off to?" he asked as she sat on the bed to put on her shoes.

"I have a couple of appointments to get settled for you," she answered. "I've been working on a small television network interview. I want to get that locked in, so I can get it penciled in for you."

"Ah, ok," he nodded his head. His eyes never left her as she gathered up her stuff and slowly walked out of the room. Her ass swished from side to side in the shorts as they walked downstairs and to the front door.

"I'll give you a call a little later," she turned and leaned to kiss his cheek. "Maybe I can come back over after Kenni is asleep and give you something to make you relax."

"That could be fun," Graylin lied. "I'll call you later tonight."

Aura smiled. It felt like her legs couldn't move fast enough, and his eyes were burning into her back. Those eyes that she fell in love with the moment she met him. She pulled open her car door and sat down. She took a deep breath and leaned her head against the steering wheel before starting up her car. As she drove away, she looked at the front door and he had been standing there watching her.

"Shit," she hissed through clenched teeth. "Shit... shit... shit!"

■■■■

"I'm here as promised, Det. Marcum," Graylin felt like he was announcing himself as he was lead into the detective's office. "What's this all about?"

"We have had to reassess our thoughts on everything surrounding you and the women in your life." Marcum stood and walked around his desk to offer his hand. He was almost surprise when Graylin accepted and shook it.

"Meaning?"

"I'm leaning towards believing that someone is attempting to frame your ex-wife for assault and murder."

"Since the death of Sadè I've been thinking along the same lines," Graylin began, "and then I got a call from another female friend of mine this morning."

"From?"

"Her name is LynMarie Craig, she lives in Houston, and undoubtedly Elise went down to visit her recently."

"When was this? Damn, is she still… alive?"

"Apparently, it was a few days ago, around the same time I was out of town visiting my… publisher." Graylin paused allowing his mind to trip back a few days before finishing his thought. "Yes, she's still alive, but she was attacked in her home. Fortunately, her husband was home and he ran off the attacker, but what was interesting was that the attacker came in through the sliding glass door."

"Yea, that is interesting," Marcum sat back nodding his head. "Anything else similar to our other cases?"

"Yea," Graylin was staring at the detective, "she was injected with pure nicotine, but just enough to put her in the hospital."

Marcum was sitting on the edge of his desk shaking his head. "Dammit. Did she happen to see her attacker?"

"That's the thing," Graylin hadn't sat down, instead he was pacing in a circle. "She didn't get a good look, but she got enough of one to tell me that the woman had dark hair, which would match Elise, but she said her eyes weren't right to her. She said that they were blue, but not a natural blue; like she was wearing contacts."

"Contacts," Marcum grunted as he stood. "Now that is interesting. Graylin, we've been missing something because we've been concentrating on Elise. The moment we realized that you hadn't beat her as she'd claim, she became my focus."

"Well granted that my ex-wife is a bit crazy," Graylin tried to chuckle that one off, "I had a problem thinking she could kill anyone. I've been told to be careful with her, and I've even told some of my female friends to be careful of her. But, that was because I just didn't want them to have to deal with confronting her. Elise is plenty loud and boisterous, I think in some ways she's even a little dangerous, but mostly to herself."

"I agree, but there's still some gaps," Graylin commented. "For one, was it ever confirmed how Trinity died? I know the initial reports were pretty much like Kaine's, stating that she died of a massive coronary."

"After I got back from Texas," Marcum pulled out another folder and flipped it open, "I called the coroner in Denver and asked if they still had some samples of her blood and asked her to do another tox-screen. Guess what she found?"

"Pure nicotine... But, Trinity wasn't killed at home. She was found in her car just outside of her office building."

"The M.O. is a little off, but what matters the most is the method of death. I'm pretty sure that if the body were to be exhumed and reexamined the M.E. would find the needle puncture mark where the nicotine was injected."

"Shit, if I was writing this," Graylin shook his head, "this would have serial killer all over it."

"Now the question is," Marcum was back to his seat going through his files, "what are we missing? What is the connecting factor that brings all of this together from her first husband, Terrence Kaine to this last lady friend of yours? What's the common denominator?"

"Me," Graylin responded. "I've always been the common denominator."

"How do you figure?"

Graylin made it to a chair and sat down. As a writer, he loved trying to unravel the mystery before the end of a book or a movie. He's always wanted to see how close to walking the right avenue he was. This mystery involves him in more ways than he was prepared to muster out, but at this point...

He had no choice.

"Start with the husband," Graylin began. "When you look at him, who does he resemble?"

Marcum's fingers were flipping through his folders searching for a picture of Terrence Kaine. He knew he had one from the coroner's office, but he was certain that he'd obtained from the police file of an earlier photograph. Pulling the photocopied image out he stared at it before looking up. How could he have missed that?

"You two could pass for brothers," his eyes going from the man in front of him and back to the image. "Not quite twins, but the resemblance if remarkable."

"I noticed that as well," Graylin said. "I looked him up and it was quite obvious to me. Slowly the puzzle has been coming together, and with each piece its lead me away from Elise. Elise is the crux, if you will; she was a victim of another kind. I just didn't understand how at first. And it began to make sense to me after I'd heard from LynMarie."

"Things started making more sense to me as well," Marcum sat back in his chair. "I took that trip to Texas because I needed more information on Kaine's death."

"And I take it that you found what you were looking for?"

"Well, actually, you helped with that. After I talked to you on the phone I realized that Elise was pretty much a victim of circumstance; she's pretty much the scapegoat of this little drama you're all tied up in. She was in Dallas, pretty much stalking you at the time that her husband was poisoned. If anyone had paid any attention to the coroner's initial timeline, they would have realized that even after the pure nicotine was found... there was no way that she could have committed the crime. Much like you being out of town when she was beaten.

"My problem remains, Graylin," Marcum stared at the man across the desk from him, "we have bodies falling around you and no one other than you as the connection."

Graylin nodded his head but said nothing more. In his head, there was a new suspect that the police hadn't considered, but how was he to prove it. If she was as smart as he was assuming she was, Aura wasn't leaving any kind of paper trail for him to pick up on. How would he even introduce yet one more woman into the mix?

His thoughts dwelled on the way Aura looked at the moment he said LynMarie's name. Her face went pale like she'd seen a ghost, and even though she played the part quite well... she was nervous. Throughout the conversation with LynMarie, Aura wouldn't look at him, and then there was her unwarranted flight. He kept hearing both LynMarie and Sadè 's voices in his head...

"Not blue, they were green..." Green as in her eyes. Aura had those cat green eyes that he'd commented on the very first time Mishelle had introduced them. Green eyes that just seemed to burn with a fire that immediately attracted him, and she had this way of batting them that would sucker him in every fucking time.

How would she have orchestrated all of this?

"Damn," he said under his breath. "Shit's about to blow up in my face, Det. Marcum, but I know who's behind this. I just have no way to prove it. I need a couple of days. Can you give me that please?"

He didn't wait for an answer as he got up and walked out of the office. His head hurt. His heart was beating a tattoo against his chest, and he was having a hard time breathing. He could see her face before his eyes, and he was unable to shake it away. He cursed himself for not seeing it all before. Who would know him better than anyone? Who was with him more than anyone? Everything pointed at Elise, but that was the cleverly planned misdirection.

"A damn fool I've been," he'd gotten out of the police precinct and was trying to draw in a few deep breaths to calm his nerves. "I should have figured this shit out long ago. Got me feeling like a fucking amateur. Not any longer."

Chapter 18: Filling in the Missing Pieces

Elise had lost count of how long she'd been crying. It could have been just hours. It was probably more like days. Her eyes burned from tears and lack of sleep. Her body hurt from being balled up in the fetal position on the sofa. Her chest and head ached. She felt like death warmed over. The images and sounds from that moment standing in his house replayed before her eyes on a continuous loop that she couldn't pause or stop. Her stomach was empty but lurched every time she heard that voice.

Oh my god, Graylin... I love you.

Her hand had found her phone and before she could stop… the phone was ringing. Elise held the phone to her ear wondering if she could really say anything. Her throat felt dry and her lips were parched as she slipped her tongue out trying to moisten them before he answered. She rolled over onto her side staring off into nothing waiting for what felt like an eternity before Graylin finally answered.

"Yea?" It always put a smile on her face whenever he answered still partially asleep. She didn't know what time it was, but there was light, so it had to be daytime.

"Hello… Graylin?" She wasn't sure how he would respond to her calling after their last face to face. "I just wanted to check on you."

"It's early still, Elise," Graylin cleared his throat. "Are you alright?"

"I…" she hesitated trying hold back the tears. "I really don't know, Graylin. I really don't know."

"What's going on, Elise?" It amazed her that he didn't sound peeved. She could feel the concern.

In her mind Elise could see him sitting up in the bed. The cover's fallen to his waist and he's sitting there with no shirt on because that's how he loved to sleep. She could see him rubbing his eyes and stretching trying to wake up. She wanted to beg him to come see her. She wanted to beg him to just lay down and hold her until she stopped crying. She wanted to scream. She wanted to…

"I was there the other day," she blurted out. "I was at your home. I was in the house and I heard…"

She could hear him rustling around in his bed and knew he'd actually sat up. He was fully awake and aware at this point, and he'd want to know.

"You were in my house?" He asked and there was that tinge of anger she'd feared. "When were you in my house, Elise? No wait, how did you get into my house?"

"That's not important, Graylin," her words were soften as she sat up on the sofa and brushed her hair from her face.

"I fucking beg to differ," he was getting angrier, but he was trying to remain calm. Elise sniffled and wiped her eyes of the fresh tears now falling. Her breathing was stuck in her throat as she tried to anticipate his next question. "When were you in my house, Elise?"

"I honestly don't know the exact day, Graylin," she answered being quite truthful. "I don't know how long I've been just laying here on my sofa. But, it was the day your 'personal assistant' Aura was there."

"You're not making any sense," Graylin was gritting his teeth. "Aura is almost always here, Elise. For the most part we're working on my schedule between writing deadlines and tours and book si--"

"And fucking," Elise interrupted. "I heard the two of you, Graylin. I heard the bitch screaming and moaning like a whore in heat. I heard her tell you that she loves you, Graylin."

"Shit," Graylin ran his hand over his head. That was two or three days ago, and the memory of it came flooding back into his memory. He hadn't known that they were not alone, but what he wanted to yell out was that she should have stayed. "You were there? Why the fuck was you there? Why the fuck was you in my goddamn house?"

He could still see Aura's face the moment he jumped up. They were both sweating and out of breath, but he was staring at her bewildered at what she'd said. She was profusely apologizing and begging for him to forgive her. Graylin was pacing at the foot of the bed ranting and raving about what had been screamed out, and the fact that their relationship was supposed to be "without any strings." He could see Aura laying there covering her naked body with the sheet from the bed but thinking about it now… she didn't seem that shocked. She didn't appear that worried or frightened.

She appeared… pleased.

"I've been in love with you for so long, Graylin," he could hear her voice, but the words were hollow… distant, "that I don't know how not to love you anymore. I've chased you. I've begged you. I've pretty much demanded that you love me back, and the only thing I've gotten in return is that you are content. You're happy not being with me anymore, and I'm sorry, Graylin, I am so sorry."

"Sorry for what?" He couldn't believe what was being said to him.

"For..." Elise took a deep breath and forced her body to stand up from the sofa, "everything. I should have done right by you when I had you, and I mistreated you. I should have respected the man I had fallen in love with and yet I spent so much time trying to make you into something that you could never be. You're a good man, Graylin, and I am so sorry that I ever hurt you."

"You have my word," Elise swallowed hard, "I'll leave you alone to your life. I'll never stop loving you, but you won't have to worry about me any longer."

"Thank you, Elise," Graylin couldn't believe what he'd just heard. "Thank you. And, Elise?"

"Yes?" she stood there smiling.

"Take care of yourself." Graylin pulled the phone his ear staring at it as he pressed the end button. He was unsure how he felt at this moment. A part of him was finally happy that she'd let go, and he was sure she'd sign the divorce papers that he'd finally filed. The other part of him wondered just how truthful she was being, and he sat there thinking that he'd look for a new house for him and Kennadey.

"Who was that?" the voice caught him off guard as he turned to see Aura rolling over to sit up. She was dressed in one of his button up dress shirts and if he knew her as well as he was sure he did... she was naked beneath the covers of his bed.

"When did you get here?" he asked turning to face her.

"It was first thing this morning," her smile was large, but he was unaffected. "I didn't want to wake you. You look so beautiful when you're sleeping."

Graylin stood from the bed. There was something not right about anything that's been going on in his life over the last few months. He sat on the edge of his dresser staring at the woman stretching in his bed. She was one of the most tempting women he'd been involved with, but the entire relationship was always supposed to be just about the sex. He was finding that there was a lot more.

Since the conversation with LynMarie, Graylin had been doing his own investigations. He was more than convinced that Elise had been Aura's patsy and now he was on the run to connect the dots together. He'd already contacted a private investigator he'd met while working on one of his books and now the man was working for him trying to dig up a few things he needed to put this shit to bed. So beautiful, but now it was looking like she was extremely dangerous. He still had to figure out her endgame; this couldn't all be about him… or could it?

"Come back to bed, Graylin," her smile was inviting. "Come and do something dirty to me."

"I wish I could," he stood there thinking of a quick lie, "but I have to go talk to the police about Sadè's death. The detective's said that he's found some new evidence and wanted to talk to me about it."

"What kind of new evidence?" Aura seemed quite interested. "Do they have a suspect?"

"I don't rightly know, but I hope so because I'm sick of being in that suspect pool."

Aura slipped from the bed and sauntered towards him. He couldn't help but notice the extra movements of her hips beneath his shirt; she was definitely naked beneath it, that much he was sure of. She draped her arms around his neck and leaned in to kiss him softly. The smell of her perfume was intoxicating, and he wasn't sure how he'd missed that earlier. He made no move to pull her into his arms. He made no effort to return her kiss, but he was staring down at her closed eyes waiting for them to open. His phone rang again, and he slipped from her arms and back to the bed to grab it and answered without looking at the screen.

"This is Cross."

"Hey, Babe," Mishelle was on the other end. "I got that information that you'd called about. Sorry it took me a bit but dealing with a lot of shit up here. There's a producer who wants something on *Deadly Ambitions* for a possible screenplay."

"That's pretty unexpected," Graylin was grinning for a moment before glancing back at Aura who was now sitting on top of the dresser. "So, what did you find for me?"

"To be honest, I'm waiting on some of this shit to be double checked on because I don't know how I missed it, but on all of those dates that you gave me…" Mishelle paused for a second, "you're right… Aura had purchased tickets to and from on the company cards. Most of them corresponded with you being in a completely different area. What the hell is this all about, Graylin?"

"I'm still trying to figure it all out," he slid his hand over his head, "but the moment I get it all figured out you'll be the first to know."

"Sounds like you have a new book on your hands to me," Mishelle laughed. "I've told you that your ass needs to slow the hell down. You're not going to kill me with all of these books."

"Yea, yea, yea," they both laughed at that. "I hear you, Boss Lady.

Look I have to go see the police about some things dealing with Sadè, so I'll give you a call later. Also, I should have the last three chapters of Tropics of Sin to you in the next few days."

"Okay," she answered. "I'm still not sure about that title, but we can deal with that later. Talk to you later, Love."

"Sounds good. I'll call soon, Sweetheart."

"Ms. Rivers?" Aura had slipped down from the dresser and was walking towards him once more.

"Yea, she's meeting with some producer about Deadly Ambitions and possibly doing a movie script for it."

"That's great, Graylin," she was completely sincere. "It's about time they recognized your talents. I've always known you'd get your books into the movies."

"True, but," he stood and headed towards the bathroom, "I need to shower and get to the police station."

As he said that, his phone buzzed, and he quickly glanced over the text message he'd just received. The P.I. was on his way over with more information for him. Now he could hopefully find what it was he was not sure that he was looking for. The investigator was digging up Aura's past, and the last thing he needed was for her to get a whiff of what he was up to. The one thing he was sure of was that she was truly a dangerous woman. Currently, she had at least three deaths under her belt, but he was sure there had to be more.

"You sure you don't want company?" Aura had unbuttoned the shirt and dropped it to the floor. Graylin had to swallow hard and turn away to keep from staring. Somewhere deep in the back of his mind were thoughts of maybe them fucking one last time, but the rational side of his mind couldn't quite cope with how sick that thought really was.

"Not today, Aura," he finally got out. "I have so much shit on my mind right now that I can't even concentrate on the small things. I need to go take care of this thing with the police and then it will be time to grab Kennadey. I really just need some time to think right now."

"Okay, Babe," she smiled as she grabbed her own clothes and began dressing. She could again feel his eyes staring at her, but it was if things between them had changed. A small part of her regretted screaming out how she felt about him, there was a reason for it, and it had helped in breaking Elise. What she hadn't wanted was for him to change his mind about her, but there was one thing she was sure of.

She could make him love her.

"Good afternoon, Mr. Cross," Horace Stanley stepped into the doorway offering his hand to Graylin. He was a rather tall fellow, balding in the top and wearing a suit that was at least two sizes too small. Graylin noticed that the man walked with an obvious limp to his left and that he also dragged that foot slightly as he stepped.

"Thanks for the text message earlier," Graylin shook the man's hand and then followed him into the living room. "Did you find anything?"

"What I found is rather strange, Sir," Horace sat on the sofa watching as Graylin sat in the arm chair just to his right. He pulled the folder he'd been holding under his arm and opened it before handing the package over to his employer.

"Strange? In what way?"

"She no more real than your second ex-wife," Horace waited for Graylin to pull out everything he'd stuffed into the envelope. "Your Aura Daniels only has a history reaching back to maybe two years before your publisher hired her to work with you. In that time, she was able to create a persona that had a strong work history going back approximately ten years, an education background, and even tax returns... but none of its real."

"Okay, so who the hell is she?"

Horace reached over and pulled out a picture. He didn't say anything as he laid the photo out for Graylin to study and he sat back waiting. He could almost see the wheels in the man's head turning much as his own had when he'd finally come across that picture. It was the only one, and he was positive that it was thought destroyed. He'd lucked out when he came across it in an old archive in Lubbock, Texas.

"Are you shitting me?" Graylin stared at the picture. His eyes had to be deceiving him, but his mind was telling him emphatically that this was no joke. "Is this real? Did you get this verified?"

"By more than once source," Horace confirmed. "The parents are still alive, Sir, not together... but they are alive. I found the mother in Amarillo; she's living with a new husband of ten years or so. The father now lives in California, single but they both verified the sisters."

"Okay, what's the story here?"

Graylin sat back in the chair staring at the picture he was holding. The two girls were just a year or so apart, maybe still in elementary school and dressed in the typical parochial school uniforms. The smaller of the two was looking up at her big sister with the biggest grin on her freckled face, and the big sister was standing with her arm gently perched atop her little sister's head. He had to choke back the bile rising up from his stomach. One was dark haired. The other was a red head.

Horace was talking. Graylin could hear him, but he wasn't listening. He was trying to wrap his mind around what was before him. He'd missed it from the very beginning, but now a lot of things were starting to make a lot of sense. The one thing he wasn't too sure about was if they both knew of the other, or if it was purely one-sided. He was banking on the later. As he studied the picture, he could see obvious differences that would make for changes as the two girls grew older.

"It appears that they were separated as children," Horace was trying to talk over the noises Graylin was dealing with in his head. "The parents could no longer take care of them and the oldest went to live with her grandmother, and the youngest was taken away by the state because she'd undoubtedly been abused by the father. When I spoke to him he told me that there were no red heads in his family and when confronted about cheating on him his wife kept demanding that he was both girls father."

"Damn," Graylin tossed the photo on the table and stood from his chair. His head felt like it was about to explode as he paced a groove into his carpet.

"Mr. Cross?" Horace watched as the man frantically walked in one direction, turned, and returned to his starting point… over and over. "Is everything alright, Sir?"

"I got my reason why," Graylin looked excited. "She fucking hates her sister. I finally got all of the pieces. There's going to be a big ass bonus in your check, Mr. Stanley. Shit, thank you for all of the work that you've done for me."

"You're welcome," Horace stood and began walking towards the door. "Is there anything else, Mr. Cross?"

"No," Graylin was still pacing. "No, we good. Thank you again."

All of his questions up to this moment were answered. Now one questioned remained… "What are you going to do now, Aura?"

Chapter 19: The Reunion

The drive from his home was in silence. Something was wrong, but Aura wasn't sure what it could be. Her thoughts were going over everything she'd put into play, and up to this point she was right where she'd figured she should be. But, something with Graylin wasn't right. Since that call with the little bitch in Houston he's been... different. She hadn't expected LynMarie to live or she would have bugged her house.

"What the fuck did you say?" she slammed her fist against the steering wheel.

. In her head she could hear the phone call Graylin had with LynMarie. LynMarie was still... alive. How was she still alive? There should have been enough of the nicotine in her bloodstream to have taken care of her. Aura was slamming her fist on the wheel again and again; she cursed at herself over and over for not finishing what she'd set out to accomplish. Now there was a possible hitch in her plans.

What if LynMarie could describe her?

"No," Aura glanced out of the windows to see if anyone had seen her and the tantrum she'd been throwing. She was at a traffic light waiting for it to turn green, and fortunately she was there alone. "No, she didn't get a chance to get a good look at me. My face was covered, and when that bitch of a husband of hers came out he was only concerned about his precious little wife lying on the floor.

What if LynMarie's husband saw her face?

"I said... No." She was screeching, and her voice was echoing through the car. "He couldn't have seen my face. He just grabbed me and threw me off of her. I got out of there before he even thought about me again."

But something is wrong. Graylin knows something. He knows something.

"What the fuck could he know? Huh?" Her questions rung inside of her head like some huge bell vibrating through her skull and echoing in her ears. "What... could he know?"

The light turned green and her path took her home. She needed to know exactly what Elise had said but knowing her as well as she did... Aura was pretty sure that her big sister had cowered down. She wanted to spit for even considering that bitch her big sister; some sister she'd turned out to be. For years after they'd been separated she'd waited. Waited for her big sister to find her. Waited for her big sister to show up at her foster home and save her from whatever atrocity she was enduring. She waited, but Elise never came.

The love she'd once known slowly became bitter. She would imagine her living with their grandmother and not as a ward of the state being moved from home to home. She'd imagine the life she could have had; she'd dreamed of it often. But, the moment she would open her eyes her reality would slap her in the face. Most times the slap was literal and usually hard enough to send her rolling across the room. At the age of eight she was pulled away from her family, and no one in her family stepped forward to stop it. She was being punished because the man she'd always known as her father was beating her because of her mother.

Family...

Aura hated her family, and as soon as this shit was taken care of with Elise she'd be dealing with her parents. She'd already decided their fates, but her big sister had to come first because she'd always loved Elise the most.

"You broke my fucking heart," she mumbled as she wiped away a tear from her eye. "Why didn't you love me like I loved you."

Maybe it's because you're not really her sister.

"What are you talking about?" Aura tried to keep her eyes on the road. "I am too her sister. That bitch she called her mom is my mom too."

But he was not your father. He's hers but you're not his. Maybe she hated you because you broke up their family.

"That was not my fault," Aura was wailing as she continued driving. Her home was close, and she was fighting to keep her head clear enough to just make it home. Could Elise have really blamed her? Was it her fault that their father was beating the shit out of her on a daily basis because his wife couldn't keep her legs closed? Why would any of that be her fault? Why? "I was born into that bullshit! I didn't cause it... I didn't cause it. He beat me."

Pulling up onto her drive way, Aura sat there staring at the front of her home. The tears were streaming from her eyes as the memories of her live before foster homes flooded her mind. She remembered all of the times with her sister and how close they were... or how close she'd always thought they were. She remembered the nicknames they'd always called one another, and how very protective her big sister had always been of her. She wanted to scream. She wanted to just jump out of her car and run through the neighborhood screaming at the top of her lungs. No one had ever loved her the way her sister had...

Pretended to love you. She never truly loved you, that was all in the mind of a child who didn't know any better.

"Stop... stop it," she began beating her head on the steering wheel. "She did love me, and when she sees me... she'll remember and then she'll be sorry. All of them are going to be sorry."

Wiping the tears from her eyes one last time, Aura steps out of the car and makes her way into her house. Her steps feel unsteady, her head was swimming and her heart was pounding hard in her chest. Her laptop was laying on the kitchen counter next to a bottle of tequila, and she smiled because a drink was definitely needed. As the computer booted up from its hibernation mode, she took that first drink and had to fight coughing. The liquor burned a path from her tongue, down her throat and into her stomach. Her chest was on fire and her eyes watered even as she filled the glass a second time.

Through blurry eyes Aura found the spy program that was set up in Elise's home and quickly found the recording from earlier with Graylin. The second drink was no better than the first and again she swallowed hard; she was not a heavy drinker, and she never drank straight alcohol because she couldn't handle the taste. Ignoring the pain in her chest Aura poured a third glass and turned on the recording; something Elise had said changed Graylin' mood and she needed to know what.

I was there the other day... I was at your home. I was in the house and I heard.

"Definitely didn't expect that from you," she muttered.

Aura had spent a lot of time and money on getting to know the woman who'd become Elise Mannsen. She knew her quirks. She knew her mannerisms. But, mostly she knew that Elise was a weak-willed woman. She found it easy to intimidate, but it was all talk. Elise was a runner. As she listened, she could hear the anger in his voice, but he was trying to control it.

You were in my house? When were you in my house, Elise? No wait, how the hell did you get into my fucking house, Elise? It was at this moment she'd awaken beside him but remained still just listening to his side of the conversation.

That's not important, Graylin.

I fucking beg to differ. When were you in my house, Elise? There was a brief pause as if she was trying to decide if she should be honest or just let it go, but finally she answered his question

I honestly don't know the exact day, Graylin. I don't know how long I've been just laying here on my sofa. But, it was the day that your personal assistant Aura was there. Aura couldn't help but smile before swallowing down her third glass of the tequila. She could hear the static tone in Elise's voice just saying her name; the woman didn't like her at all, but little did she know her hate paled in comparison to the hatred Aura felt towards her.

You're not making any sense, Aura is almost always here, Elise. For the most part we're working on my schedules between writing deadlines and tours and book signings. Graylin paused as if thinking of something else that Aura was there with him doing, but his thoughts were interrupted.

And fucking... I heard the two of you, Graylin. I heard the bitch screaming and moaning like a whore in heat. I heard her screaming out telling you that she... that she loves you, Graylin. I heard her. I fucking heard her.

Shit...

Aura could hear Elise crying and her smile broadened. She wanted Elise to hurt, but this felt better. The sound of her crying was better than seeing her face in the video from that day, but her pains were just beginning. The conversation toned down for a moment, and she could tell that he felt sorry for her.

Aura could feel the intoxicating effects of the tequila. She stood there laughing at Elise as she poured one more shot of tequila into her glass. She rewound the part where Elise was trying to explain her love to Graylin, and with each word her laughter grew louder.

You're happy not being with me anymore, and I'm sorry, Graylin. I am so sorry.

Sorry for what? Aura was a little shocked. She hadn't expected this from Elise. Nothing that she'd learned about this woman would have even suggested that she would be willing to blame herself for the shit she'd put anyone through, and yet...

For... everything. I should have done right by you when I had you, but instead, I mistreated you. I should have respected the man that I had fallen in love with and yet I spent so much time trying to make you into something that you could never be. You're a good man, Graylin, and I am so sorry that I ever hurt you. You have my word... I'll leave you alone to your life.

"No... No!" Aura had grabbed the bottle of tequila and it was thrown across the room where it shattered against the far wall of the dining room. "You will not take this away from me, you stupid bitch."

Elise sat at the kitchen counter staring off into space. For her the last few days had been a trying few days, but at this moment she felt good. The conversation with Graylin this morning had actually helped to clear her conscious. Her obsession for him she had her doubts would ever go away. She'd told him honestly that she would always love him and that's exactly how she felt.

She smiled as she pulled a bottle of wine from the refrigerator. It was a crisp, fruity Moscato that she'd come to enjoy, and after the time that she'd put into getting her house cleaned up a drink was definitely needed. It was deserved. She poured a glass and stood there humming to the music softly playing through the speakers. Looking around she almost laughed at how much she still needed to do.

"I cannot believe this shit," she grinned. "Wait, yes I can."

"So, can I."

The sound of another voice startled her, and she dropped the glass of wine she'd just picked up. Looking up from the shattered mess on her kitchen floor the first thing that caught her attention was not the person, but the barrel of the pistol that was pointed in her direction. Her breath caught in her throat and her hand immediately covered her mouth. Her eyes bugged, and she had to force them past the front of the gun to the person standing behind it.

"A...Aura?"

"Hello, Nene," Aura's smile was huge. Her eyes were glazed from the tequila, and her hand was shaking noticeably.

"What did you just call me?" Elise's voice trembled.

"I called you what I used to always call you, Nina," Aura stepped forward so that Elise could clearly see her in the light from the kitchen. "I called you what I always called my big sister."

"Big... sister?" Elise stood staring at the other woman completely confused. "I... I... don't understand. What do you mean?"

The words were there, they'd been said, but not understood. Elise had had a sister long ago. Long before she'd changed her name. Long before she'd changed her past, but that little girl had been killed in a car accident shortly after they'd been separated. She remembered clearly the day that her mother had come to visit her at her grandmother's home. She remembered; every word her mother had said rattled around in her head as it has since she was about ten years old.

Janine, baby, mommy has some really bad news for you. That was how her mother had started it just after she'd had her little girl sit down on the sofa beside her. Her mother had tears in her eyes, and beneath her eyes were all red and swollen like she'd been crying for a while. *Your little sister… Janice has…*

"What don't you understand, Nene?" Aura stood in front of her with the barrel of the pistol almost touching her forehead. Her smile was huge, spreading from ear to ear. Her eyes were wide as she stared at the confused woman she'd grown up to hate. "What is there to understand, Big Sister? I mean when you put all of the pieces together, you have to understand that I… fucking… hate you, Janine."

The words were like a knife through her heart. Elise couldn't take her eyes off of the woman she'd grown to despise because of her relationship with her husband. But, to find out that this very same woman was the sister that she'd thought she'd lost when she was just a child was overwhelming.

"Mommy said that you had…" the words caught in her throat and her breath hung in her chest. "I thought that you had…"

"Had what, Nene," Aura spat out the words. "HAD WHAT."

"Died, Nieci!" Elise screamed as her knees buckled. She had to grab onto the counter top to keep from dropping to the floor into the broken glass and wine. "Mommie said that you'd died."

Aura was frozen in place as the words that fell from her sister's lips vibrated inside of her head. For close to fifteen years; fifteen long years she'd waited to stand before her sister again, and for the majority of that she'd come to terms with wanting to just kill her. She'd learned to live with the fact that she was alone in this world. She'd come to live with the fact that her father wasn't her father, her mother wasn't her mother, and the one person in this world that she loved… didn't love her back. This was her crux. This had become her reason for recreating the person she'd become. This had been the reason she'd…

Killed.

Aura looked at her hands. They were covered in blood. Blood of the last foster parents she'd had because the husband has used her for his own personal sex toy. She'd become used to being mistreated. She gotten used to being abused. She understood that she wasn't meant to be loved because Janine had stopped loving her. So that last night when he'd come into her room she was ready. She'd made plans on how she was going to kill him and then his wife would be next because she knew what he was doing.

He came to her bed and she was already naked. She wasn't quite sixteen. She was scared but she was sick of this slimy, greasy smelling pig slipping into her bed and forcing her legs open. Tonight, she wanted him to come to her, and he did. He was drunk. He was loud, and the television in the living room was still on… that mean the wife was still up. He slammed the door open and didn't even bother to close it as he removed his clothes as he walked into her room. His dick hung limply between his hairy legs slowly stiffening, and she waited. He pulled the covers back and she was ready for him; naked with her legs spread wide and her arms reaching out for him.

"Oh, look at you," he grinned and wiped a dirty hand over his wet lips, "all open and ready for me. 'Bout time you got used to this, little Bitch."

She watched as she stroked himself hard before dropping between her thighs. He grunted as he pushed his way into her body. He grunted harder as he began to pump and pound between her thighs. She'd wrapped her legs around him and locked her feet at the ankles, and she just lay there allowing him to do his business. She waited, slipping her hand under the pillow and wrapping her small hand around the hilt of the butcher's knife hidden there. She watched his face trying to fight the gurgling bubbles building in her stomach that threatened to make her vomit all over the both of them.

She watched him, and she waited.

"OH…" he growled into her ear as he pressed his full weight down on her boy. "I'm there… I'm ther…"

His words trailed off as the knife struck him once in the side and then again in back. She was rolling with him as he tried to roll off of her and she pressed her mouth to his before he could call out to the woman sitting in the living room. The knife struck him in the side of his chest and then quickly in his neck before she sat up on his body. She wanted to laugh as his body jerked and spasmed beneath her. Leaning over him, she stared into his eyes as the blood bubbled in his mouth. He was trying to mouth words, but only a strangled gurgling sound babbled forward.

"I bet you don't love me anymore," she whispered into hear. "Do you, you fucking bastard.?"

As his eyes darkened, his body stopped moving. Taking a deep breath, Janice jumped up from the body and ran into the bathroom to vomit. There was much in her stomach to bring up, and the bile that followed burned like acid causing her eyes to water. The knife had been left in the man's throat, and she'd need it. Wiping her eyes and smearing the blood on her hands across her face, she made it back into the room to retrieve her weapon.

"You're next, Bitch," she smiled as she walked from the room still naked into the living room.

There was so much blood on her hands. She stood watching as Elise leaned against the counter crying and trying to keep her body from falling to the floor. Her big sister's words were on a continuous loop telling her over and over that their mother had to lied to the older girl. Their mother.

"You, lying bitch," Aura swung out with her empty hand striking Elise hard against her cheek and jaw. She watched as the woman bounced off the counter and flopped to the floor in a heap just barely missing the broken glass. Her foot struck out catching Elise in the stomach causing her to fold up and slump into a fetal position with her head covered by her arms and her legs crouched up into her stomach.

"I hate you," Aura was crouched down beside her sister. "I hate you, and none of that bullshit is fucking true. You know it ain't and I know it ain't."

"But it is, Aura," the man's voice was too familiar to be mistaken. "Every word of it is very true."

Chapter 20: Full Circle and a New Story to Come

"Graylin?" Aura slowly stood pointing the pistol in the direction of the voice. "What are you doing here?"

"It took me a moment to figure it all out," Graylin stepped into the kitchen and glanced down at Elise lying on the floor. He slowly eased his way around the counter and past Aura to stand over his ex-wife.

"I didn't want to believe the shit that I found out, but I'd paid some really good money for the shit that I got. But, I must admit… it was hard to swallow no matter how I tried to wrap my head around it."

Graylin acted as if the gun being pointed at him didn't exist as he knelt down to check Elise. She fought him for a second before realizing that it wasn't her sister trying to get in another swing at her face. She looked up into the dark brown eyes of the one person she thought she couldn't love any harder, and then looked past him to stare into the green eyes of the woman she'd never realized was the little sister she'd lost. Elise whimpered as the pain in her stomach caused the muscles to contract as Graylin helped her to sit up against the stove.

"Why are you here?" Elise finally formed the words.

"Well here's the thing," Graylin stood and found the cabinet with the glass and filled one with water from the sink before handing the glass to Elise, "I got the information about the two of you from my private investigator this morning after I'd finally gotten Aura out of my house."

"She was there this morning?" Elise asked after taking a sip of the water. "Was she there when I called you?"

"Why of course I was," Aura gloated. "I was naked except for his shirt asleep in his bed. And we were about to…"

"About to nothing, Aura," Graylin cut his eyes at her stopping her words before she continued. "We were about to nothing, because there hadn't been anything since that day."

Aura stared at him and her eyes glowed with a renewed anger.

"Just from the look, and the fact that I now know that Elise was there," Graylin leaned back against the counter crossing his arms, "I know that you planned it all. You knew because you'd sent her… hadn't you, Aura? You pretty much had that shit timed out and I knew from the moment that I jumped up that something about that entire moment was all fucked up."

"What are you talking about, Graylin?" Aura tried to soften her words. Her eyes glazed with tears as she looked from him to Elise still sitting on the floor.

"All of it was bullshit," Graylin turned and stared at the red-haired woman he'd shared his bed with on a regular basis. "All of it. From the moment that you were introduced to me, I was just a pawn in your little game."

"No," Aura was shaking her head. "No, you're wrong, Graylin. I swear to you that you're wrong."

"You don't love me, Aura. Or should I call you... Janice?"

Reaching down, Graylin finally helped Elise from the floor. He led her into the dining room and pulled out a chair for her to sit down. He brushed her hair from her face and checked the burning red mark at her cheek. He shook his head and leaned in to kiss the handprint left by Aura on her sister's face.

"My investigator spoke to your parents, Girls," it was said like an announcement. "I now understand why you went through all of this trouble, Aura; now it all makes sense to me. This whole time, I'd been missing that one piece that made it all make some kind of sense to me. I mean... as a writer of this kind of shit, the pieces had to fit into the puzzle some kind of way to make ONE cohesive picture. I couldn't figure that part out. I was getting bits and pieces, but where was the cotter pin?"

"You're rambling," Aura said waving the gun. "What are you getting at?"

"Simple this," Graylin reached into the pocket of his jacket and pulled out something passing it to Elise. He smiled as her face lit up at the picture she sat there holding.

"What is that?" Aura stepped up trying to look around Graylin. She accepted the picture from Elise and stared at it a moment. "Where the fuck did you get this?"

"I'm sure that you thought you had everything taken care of, Aura," Graylin stepped from between the two sisters. "A lot of looking went into finding that picture, and then even more looking into finding your mom. And your dad."

Both stared at him. Graylin was all smiles. "Like I said it took a moment for the pieces to fit together, but I figured it out. Love."

"What does that mean, Graylin?" Elise asked.

"She's pissed at you because she loves you, Elise." Graylin pointed to the picture. "You are the one person she thought loved her all of those years ago. I mean, you thought that Elise was going to find you and save you... am I right?"

"You don't know what the fuck you're talking about," Aura raised the gun pointing back at Graylin, but he didn't flinch.

"I think I'm right on target," Graylin smiled. "All of this points to the fact that you thought your big sister had forgotten about you. You go after her first husband and you kill him."

Elise turned to Aura and stepped away slowly. "You killed Terrence? But… why?"

"Probably for the same reason that you married him, Elise," Graylin never took his eyes off of the gun pointed in his direction. "Me. You married him because he looked like me, and she killed him because he looked too much like me.

"She knew he didn't make you happy and so, she set up for you and me to naturally cross paths. You ever wonder how you won the tickets that you got for that Dallas convention? When I checked all of the records… it had been sold out for weeks. And then there was the meeting at the bookshop in Atlanta. It was all orchestrated so very well."

"You need to shut the fuck up, Graylin," the threat was obvious coming from Aura. "You have no idea what you're talking about."

"But I do," Graylin was sitting on the back of the sofa with his arms crossed over his chest. "Think about Elise, you're led to these women I know and suddenly things are pointing at you as the murderer. I called Mishelle, Aura, and as smart as you are you were really rather stupid using the company credit cards to book your flights to Denver and Houston.

"But your biggest mistakes… the pure nicotine and the contacts; both Sadè and LynMarie saw your eyes."

Throwing the picture down on the table Aura began pacing. Both hands were at her head and she was beating her fists at her temples. Too much had gone into all of this planning and the man she'd finally wanted to truly give herself to was sitting here tearing everything apart. She stopped and stared at Graylin. His look was so smug like he had a secret he'd yet to tell. Her hands came down and she once again pointed the gun towards his face.

"Why the fuck are you here, Graylin?" Her voice trembled with a burning anger that now accosted her. "You're ruining everything… why did you have to come here?"

"What's going o…" Before she could finish her question, Aura had back handed her hard spinning her towards the table.

"Shut up, you bitch." Aura turned back to face Graylin once more. "I wanted you to love me, you know, I figured that after a while you would love me."

"There was never that kind of love between us, Aura," he stood and walked up on her. "I have always cared about you, loved you in a way, but I have never been in love with you. It was supposed to be without strings… remember?"

"Yea, but…" Aura shook her head trying not to hear what he was saying to her.

"No buts, Aura," he reached out and touched her face softly. "I guess I should have guessed this shit a long time ago, but I was so wrapped up in bunch of other shit."

"No," she looked up at him with tears in her eyes, "not other shit, you mean those other bitches you were sleeping with. You didn't fucking need them, Graylin, you had me. I could have taken care of you. I wanted to take care of you."

"Aura, you saw the shit I was dealing with between Elise and I," he turned his back and stepped back to the sofa, "I didn't want to jump right back into anything serious. I just wanted to live for a while."

Elise stood listening. Her face stung and as she licked her bottom lip she could taste a faint hint of blood. She couldn't tear her eyes from Aura's face. All of the years she'd been with her husband, this woman had been there as well calling herself his personal assistant. In her mind she kept wondering if they'd been sleeping together the entire time.

"Why didn't you," she finally spoke up. "Why didn't you just tell me who you were, Nieci? Why didn't you just come to me?"

"Come to you…" Aura began laughing. "Why the fuck would I come to you? You forgot about me. You went on with your little life and you forgot all about me."

"She told me that you had died," Elise reached to touch her little sister. "I thought that you were dead. Do you know how long I mourned for you? Do You? Do you know that I spent an entire year not talking?"

"Do you know that I spent years getting passed from foster home to foster home?" Aura quickly countered. "Do you know, Janine, that I spent years getting raped by one foster father after a-fucking-nother? Did you fucking know that?"

Graylin took a quick glance at his watch. He'd called Marcum after he'd dropped Kennadey off at this parents' home. He knew what he had to do, but the question remained… would the cops hear her confession. He was stalling for time with no way of knowing if he was up to his ears in shit alone. He glanced at Elise as she stared still not believing that the sister she'd thought dead all of these years was standing right there in front of her.

"I'm sorry, Nieci," Elise's voice was pleading her to believe her. "God if I'd known... I just didn't know."

"She's not lying, Aura," Graylin interjected. "My investigator got the same story from the mother, and the father just didn't give a fuck. He swore up and down that that your mother had cheated on him."

"Yea," Aura's head spun to stare at him, "I remember the argument. I remember all of the yelling and the screaming. I remember that fat ass bastard calling her a slut, and she swore that there hadn't been anyone else. But don't you worry..."

Aura smiled. Her head was hurting from the alcohol and the situation. She'd never heard this story about her being dead. She'd definitely have to get her money back from that asshole of an investigator she'd hired. She closed her eyes trying to clear her head enough to think, but everything was too jumbled.

"So much... blood," she mumbled. "Why so much..."

"Aura," Graylin called her name causing her to stop waving the pistol around. "Aura, I need to know something."

"Huh?" Aura slowly walked back towards the sliding glass door. She felt hot. Her body felt as if it were set on a low boil and steaming. She wanted to open the door and get some air into the room just to cool off.

"Aura," his voice was deep and demanding causing her body to shiver as she turned from the window to stare at him once more. His face was beautiful to her. Those big brown eyes staring at her never ceased to make her body jump from the inside out. She's kissed those delicious full lips so many times that she knew every crease in them by heart. His hands were large and with just a thought she could feel them all over her body kneading and fondling her towards an orgasm.

"Aura," Graylin repeated her name, "I need to ask you something... okay?"

"Of course, Babe," she smiled at him not fully aware that she'd raised the gun at him once more. "What do you need to know?"

"I get Trinity, I understand why you killed her, and I even understand why you went after LynMarie," Graylin knew that he was treading dangerous waters. "Why Sadè? Why my daughter's mom?"

Aura froze in place. Why was he asking her that? She stared at him, but his facial expression hadn't changed. His eyes felt as if they were boring into her skull, and it was making her nervous. She turned and took a look outside, but there was nothing out in the dark that looked out of place. Why had he asked her that? Why would he want to know?

"I don't understand why..." she felt confused. Her stomach was suddenly doing flip flops and her heart was pounding so hard that she felt dizzy. "You're trying to… trick me, or something. Why are you asking me that, Graylin?"

"Why wouldn't I, Aura," Graylin shrugged his shoulders. "We both know that it wasn't Elise, and we both equally know that it was you. Now, I honestly don't see either Elise or myself getting out of here alive, so, I want to know why you killed Sadè?"

"Stop… stop," she was shaking her head violently. "You're trying to fuck with me. I'm not this bitch over here, you… you can't make me feel stupid. So, what are you asking me that?"

The sound of her pulling back the hammer echoed, and Elise gasped. Aura locked her elbow as she held the gun unwavering at Graylin. She cocked her head and smiled. She was in control, and him with his smooth, suave voice would not sway her. Slowly she turned her aim towards Elise.

"Tell me, or my big sister gets it between those pretty blue eyes."

"I've already told you why," Graylin remained calmed. He remained sitting on the back of the sofa and he kept his eyes on hers. As a writer, he'd learned during all of his research that quick, sudden moves could cause the assailant to strike out. He wanted her to remain calm, but mostly he wanted her attention on him.

"Point that back this way and talk to me." He watched as she stared at him. Her eyes were glazed, and again filling with tears "I just want to know why her?"

"She wanted you back, Graylin," Aura answered as tears slowly rolled from her eyes. "I could see it in her eyes. She was willing to take a step back into your life and she would have said it was for Kennadey's benefits. She was going to use your baby against you, and since you had left this bitch… Sadè knew she could get you back. I couldn't let that happen.

"Sadè had to die. Trinity was triflin and disrespectful… the way she talked to Nene when she went to talk to her… well she wasn't meant to even be a part of your life. She thought that she mattered when all she was, was a piece of ass to you. Out of all of them… I enjoyed watching that bitch die."

"That's all I needed to know," Graylin said as he slowly stood from the sofa. Reaching into his jacket pocket he pulled out his cell phone and turned it to face Aura. He watched as her eyes stretched. Over the speaker of the phone they could all hear the voices. "It's the police, Aura. They're right outside and they're about to come up in here. Drop the gun."

"You son-of-a-bitch…" Aura shrieked as she leveled the gun towards his face. "I fucking hate you… I FUCKING HATE YOU!"

Graylin never expected to see the burst of fire from the muzzle of the gun. His heart leaped into his throat as he turned hoping against hope that he was faster than the bullet he could only imagine soaring from the tip of the pistol. He screamed out, but that was too late as the molten lead struck his body throwing him over the sofa. He bounced off the cushions and onto the floor. The legs of the coffee table stopped him from rolling, and he looked up to see if she was standing over him. His eyes dimmed. He could hear the police rushing into the room. His ears were ringing. He could smell something like burnt meat. His stomach coiled, and he felt like he was about to vomit.

She'd actually shot him.

"Fuck," he said weakly as he felt his breathing whispering between his lips. "Fuck."

"Mr. Cross? Mr. Cross, can you hear me?" The voice sounded distant and hollow as the room around him grew dark.

"Graylin! Hold on, we got an emergency crew com…"

■■■■

"Daddy?"

The sound of Kennadey's voice played in his head like an angel's harp. He wanted to reach out for her and touch her face one last time. He could see her over him smiling down. His beautiful little angel.

"Daddy, are you okay?" her voice sounded closer. "Daddy?"

"Yea, Kenni, I'm okay." He could hear his response, but he didn't feel his lips moving.

Opening his eyes hurt thanks to the bright lights. He would have thought that he was in heaven if it hadn't been for the beeping that was just to his right. He tried to blink the lights down to a more tolerable level, and this dried his pupils. A slight grunt escaped his parched lips as he tried to move. He wasn't on the floor. The rustle of sheets confirmed that he was in a bed as he gingerly turned his head trying to look around.

"Take it easy, Graylin," the voice was female, but he didn't recognize it right off. The lights didn't dim any, but he as slowly getting used to them. The room was a little blurry, but he immediately recognized that he was in a hospital room. That made the beeping noises obvious. That also made the antiseptic smell that as assailing his smell obvious.

"I'm not dead?" The question was for whoever was in the room as his gaze turned towards the open window to his far right. It was daylight, and it was beautiful. He tried to move again and the sharp pain in the crook of his left arm stopped him. He was stiff all over and he was dying for something to drink.

"No, you're not dead yet," Mishelle stepped around the bed so that he could see her. "If that crazy female hadn't been hit by the other crazy female you probably would be."

"Goddamn, I'm hurting all over," Graylin tried to laugh. "Good to see you though, Boss Lady."

"Good to see your ass too," Mishelle leaned over and kissed his cheek. "You scared the shit out all of us. And, after I heard what you did… well, let's just say I wanted to kick your ass."

Graylin began laughing but stopped because it hurt his chest. He looked down his body, but the sheets had him covered up, so he couldn't see anything. He took a deep breath and cough as he quickly released it. "Where was I…"

"She got you in the chest," Mishelle reached out touching the right side of his chest. "Elise tried to stop her, but the gun went off and as you turned the bullet struck you just to the right of your sternum. The doctor said a few inches more to the right and you may have lost a lung… a little more towards the left and it would have hit your heart. You were lucky."

"Yea, lucky me." Graylin looked up at his friend and publisher. "I heard my daughter… I thought I heard Kennadey."

"I told your family that I would sit with you for a while," Mishelle held his glass for him to take a sip of his water. "You've been in and out for almost a week. They've pretty much been here that entire time, so I asked them to go home and get some rest."

"Thank you," he looked towards the door and saw that it was closed. "Mishelle, what happened to Aura and Elise?"

"Elise walked away without as much as a scratch," Mishelle shook her head. "Goddamn, Graylin, I didn't know you had all of this shit going on around you down here. Do I need to move down here to keep your ass out of trouble?"

"Most likely," he chuckled softly and then waited for her to continue.

"Aura… damn, I can't believe I trusted that one," Mishelle sat on the edge of the bed. "She's currently in county awaiting her first hearing. The D.A. was pretty much waiting to see how you were going to do before taking further actions. As far as I can tell, she's being held without bail with three counts of first degree murder and at least two counts of attempted, and they're adding in aggravated assault with a firearm for good measures. Her ass ain't getting out of there for a while."

Graylin nodded his head. In his mind he was sadden because the woman he'd known for the last few years was not the woman who had attempted to shoot him. He was mad at himself because he'd missed that side of her, and somehow, she'd been able to pull the wool over his eyes on a number of things. At some point he would need to apologize to Elise for believing she was the one responsible for the deaths.

"I'm thinking I want to move Kennadey away from all of this," he said. "I think we both need a new start, and with everything that I've been through I just don't think I want to go back into that house."

"I don't blame you," Mishelle grinned trying to lighten his spirits. "But, look at it this way... with all of this shit that you've just gone through, you have yourself one Hellava book on your hands. I think you need to get started writing it."

"Yea," he smiled as what she said bounced around in his head. "Shit, you're right, all of this would make one hellava best seller."

About the Author

Gerald R Johnson has been a writer from an early age, and it began with his love of ready that his parents instilled in him at about 3 years old. Fantasy stories were his primary genre of choice because it would allow him to disappear to become anything from a knight to a barbarian to a wizard. He wrote his first complete novel when he was around 16, but... he was hooked. His English teachers in high school recognized his talents to weave tales with his words and pushed him to reach higher with his composition content and kept him enthusiastic about writing more.

Gerald has always felt that the primary purpose of writing was to entertain, not only himself, but most definitely others. It took him years to finally see to it that others got to share in the joy and love that he has for writing. Growing up, few people were privileged to read his work, and even though he was given the rave reviews he'd dreamed of, Gerald was still "shy" about sharing his writing. Fast Forward to about 8 years ago and all of that changed when he published his first two books, *Pitch Darke: the Poetic Chronicles of Damien Darke* and *Liquid Eroticism*. Since then he has had his first urban series, the Tainted series, published, and he's looking forward to sharing some new work in the very near future.

www.ingramcontent.com/pod-product-compliance
Lightning Source LLC
Chambersburg PA
CBHW021149080526
44588CB00008B/270